MW01627183

# The NIV Study Bible

## New International Version

# Gospel of John

General Editor
KENNETH BARKER

Associate Editors
DONALD BURDICK
JOHN STEK
WALTER WESSEL
RONALD YOUNGBLOOD



Zondervan Publishing House
GRAND RAPIDS, MICHIGAN 49530, U.S.A.

The Gospel of John


From the NIV® Study Bible

Printed in the United States of America

# Introduction

## *About the Study Bible*

The New International Version of the Bible is unsurpassed in accuracy, clarity and literary grace. The commitments that led to the completion of this version later guided several of its translators to spearhead publication of *The NIV Study Bible.* Their purpose was unchanged: to communicate the word of God to the hearts of people.

Like the NIV itself, *The NIV Study Bible* is the work of a transdenominational team of Biblical scholars. All confess the authority of the Bible as God's infallible word to humanity. They have sought to clarify understanding of, develop appreciation for, and provide insight into that word.

But why a study Bible when the NIV text itself is so clearly written? Surely there is no substitute for the reading of the text itself; nothing people write *about* God's word can be on a level with the word itself. Further, it is the Holy Spirit alone—not fallible human beings—who can open the human mind to the divine message.

However, the Spirit also uses people to explain God's word to others. It was the Spirit who led Philip to the Ethiopian eunuch's chariot, where he asked, "Do you understand what you are reading?" (Ac 8:31). "How can I," the Ethiopian replied, "unless someone explains it to me?" Philip then showed him how an Old Testament passage in Isaiah related to the good news of Jesus.

This interrelationship of the Scriptures—so essential to understanding the complete Biblical message —is a major theme of the Study Bible notes.

Doctrinally, the Study Bible reflects traditional evangelical theology. Where editors were aware of significant differences of opinion on key passages or doctrines, they tried to follow an evenhanded approach by indicating those differences (e.g., see note on Rev 20:2). In finding solutions to problems mentioned in the book introductions, they went only as far as evidence (Biblical and non-Biblical) could carry them.

The result is a study Bible that can be used profitably by all Christians who want to be serious Bible students.

## *Features of the NIV Study Bible*

*The NIV Study Bible* features the text of the New International Version, study notes keyed to and listed with Bible verses, introductions and outlines to books of the Bible, text notes, a cross-reference system (100,000 entries), parallel passages, a concordance (over 35,000 references), charts, maps, essays and comprehensive indexes.

The text of the NIV, which is divided into paragraphs as well as verses, is organized into sections with headings.

### *Study Notes*

The outstanding feature of this Study Bible is its nearly 20,000 study notes located on the same pages as the verses and passages they explain.

The study notes provide new information to supplement that found in the NIV text notes. Among other things, they

1. explain important words and concepts (see note on Lev 11:44 about "holiness");
2. interpret "difficult verses" (see notes on Mal 1:3 and Lk 14:26 for the concept of "hating" your parents);
3. draw parallels between specific people and events (see note on Ex 32:30 for the parallels between Moses and Christ as mediators);
4. describe historical and textual contexts of passages (see note on 1Co 8:1 for the practice of eating meat sacrificed to idols); and
5. demonstrate how one passage sheds light on another (see note on Ps 26:8 for how the presence of God's glory marked his presence in the tabernacle, in the temple, and finally in Jesus Christ himself).

Some elements of style should be noted:

1. Study notes on a *passage* precede notes on individual verses within that passage.
2. When a book of the Bible is referred to within a note on that book, the book name is not repeated. For example, a reference to 2 Timothy 2:18 within the notes on 2 Timothy is written 2:18, not 2Ti 2:18.

3. In lists of references within a note, references from the book under discussion are placed first. The rest appear in Biblical order.

*Introductions to Books*

Each introduction to each book of the Bible is different. Introductions vary in length and reflect both the nature of the material itself and the strengths and interests of contributing editors.

An introduction frequently reports on a book's title, author, and date of writing. It details the book's background and purpose, explores themes and theological significance, and points out special problems and distinctive literary features. Where appropriate, such as in Paul's letters to the churches, it describes the original recipients of a book and the city in which they lived.

A complete outline of the book's content is provided in each introduction (except for the introduction to Psalms). For Genesis, two outlines—a literary and a thematic—are given. Pairs of books that were originally one literary work, such as 1 and 2 Samuel, 1 and 2 Kings, and 1 and 2 Chronicles, are outlined together.

*Text Notes*

NIV text notes are indicated by raised, bold-faced letters following the words or phrases they explain. They examine such things as alternate translations, meanings of Hebrew and Greek terms, Old Testament quotations, and variant readings in ancient Biblical manuscripts. Text notes appear at the bottom of the right-hand column, preceded by their bold letters and verse numbers.

*Cross-Reference System*

The cross-reference system can be used to explore concepts, as well as specific words. For example, one can either study "angels as protectors" (see Mt 18:10) or focus on the word "angel" (see Jn 20:12).

The NIV cross-reference system resembles a series of interlocking chains with many links. The head, or organizing, link in each concept chain is indicated by the letter "S" (short for "See"). The appearance of a head link in a list of references usually signals another list of references that will cover a slightly different aspect of the concept or word being studied. The various chains in the cross-reference system—which is virtually inexhaustible—continually intersect and diverge.

Cross references are indicated by raised light-italic letters. When a single word is addressed by both text notes and cross references, the bold NIV text-note letter comes first. The cross references normally appear in the center column and, when necessary, continue at the bottom of the right-hand column preceding the NIV text notes.

The lists of references are in Biblical order with one exception: If reference is made to a verse within the same chapter, that verse (indicated by "ver") is listed first. If an Old Testament verse is quoted in the New Testament, the New Testament reference is marked with an asterisk (*).

Genesis 1:1 provides a good example of the resources of the cross-reference system.

*The Beginning*

1 In the beginning[a] God created[b]
the heavens[c] and the earth.[d] 2Now
the earth was[a] formless[e] and emp-
ty,[f] darkness was over the surface
of the deep,[g] and the Spirit of God[h]
was hovering[i] over the waters.

3And God said,[j] "Let there be light," and
there was light.[k] 4God saw that the
light was good,[l] and he separated
the light from the darkness.[m] 5God
called[n] the light "day," and the
darkness he called "night."[o] And
there was evening, and there was
morning[p]—the first day.

**1:1** [a]Ps 102:25; Pr 8:23; Isa 40:21; 41:4, 26; Jn 1:1-2 [b]ver 21,27; Ge 2:3 [c]ver 6; Ne 9:6; Job 9:8; 37:18; Ps 96:5; 104:2; 115:15; 121:2; 136:5; Isa 40:22; 42:5; 51:13; Jer 10:12; 51:15 [d]Ge 14:19; 2Ki 19:15; Ne 9:6; Job 38:4; Ps 90:2; 136:6; 146:6; Isa 37:16; 40:28; 42:5; 44:24; 45:12,18; Jer 27:5; 32:17; Ac 14:15; 17:24; Eph 3:9; Col 1:16; Heb 3:4; 11:3; Rev 4:11; 10:6 **1:2** [e]Isa 23:1;

The four lists of references all relate to creation, but each takes a different perspective. Note *a* takes up the time of creation: "in the beginning." Note *b* lists three other occurrences of the word "created" in Genesis 1-2. Note *c* focuses on "the heavens" as God's creation. Because note *d* is attached to the end of the verse as well as to the word "earth," it deals with the word "earth," with the phrase "the heavens and the earth" and with creation itself (the whole verse).

*Parallel Passages*

When two or more passages of Scripture are nearly identical or deal with the same event, this "parallel" is noted at the sectional headings for those passages. Such passages are especially common in Matthew, Mark, Luke and John, and in Samuel, Kings and Chronicles.

Identical or nearly identical passages are noted with *"pp."* Similar passages—those not dealing with the same event—are noted with *"Ref."*

To conserve space and avoid repetition, when a parallel passage is noted at a sectional heading, no further parallels are listed in the cross-reference system.

*Concordance*

The concordance is the largest ever bound together with an English Bible. By looking up key words, you can find verses for which you remember a word or two but not their location. For example, to find the verse that states that the word of God is "sharper than any double-edged sword," you could look in the concordance under either "sharper," "double-edged," or "sword."

*Maps*

The Study Bible includes 60 maps: 16 full color and 44 black and white. The 16 full-color maps at the end of this Bible cover nearly 4,000 years of history, from the patriarchs to Jerusalem today.

Strategically placed throughout the text are almost four dozen black-and-white maps specially designed for the Study Bible. The Contents contains a complete list of the topics covered.

The cities of Damascus, Rome, Corinth, Ephesus and Philippi have been reconstructed as they might have been in New Testament times. These recreations allow Bible students to visualize the places through which Paul traveled on his missionary journeys.

*Charts*

Complementing the study notes are 35 charts, diagrams and drawings designed specifically for the Study Bible. Two full-color time lines, located in the front of this Bible, pinpoint significant dates in the Old and New Testaments. Other charts, carefully placed within the text, give detailed information about ancient non-Biblical texts, about Old Testament covenants, sacrifices, and feast days, about Jewish sects, and about major archaeological finds relating to the New Testament.

*Essays*

Four brief essays give additional information on specific sections of the Bible: the Minor Prophets, the Synoptic Gospels, the Pastoral Letters, and the General Letters.

A fifth essay details the history, literature and social developments of the 400 years between the Old and New Testaments.

*Subject and Map Indexes*

The subject index pinpoints other references to persons, places, events and topics mentioned in the Study Bible notes.

Two map indexes help in locating place-names on a map.

# Contributors

| | |
|---|---|
| General Editor: | Kenneth L. Barker |
| Associate Editors: | Donald W. Burdick<br>John H. Stek<br>Walter W. Wessel<br>Ronald Youngblood |

The individuals named below contributed and/or reviewed material for *The NIV Study Bible*. However, since the General Editor and the Associate Editors extensively edited the notes on most books, they alone are responsible for their final form and content.

The chief contributors of original material to the Study Bible are listed first. Where the Associate Editors and General Editor contributed an unusually large number of notes on certain books, their names are also listed.

|  |  |
|---|---|
| Genesis | Ronald Youngblood |
| Exodus | Ronald Youngblood; Walter C. Kaiser, Jr. |
| Leviticus | R. Laird Harris; Ronald Youngblood |
| Numbers | Ronald B. Allen; Kenneth L. Barker |
| Deuteronomy | Earl S. Kalland; Kenneth L. Barker |
| Joshua | Arthur Lewis |
| Judges | John J. Davis; Herbert Wolf |
| Ruth | Marvin R. Wilson; John H. Stek |
| 1,2 Samuel | J. Robert Vannoy |
| 1,2 Kings | J. Robert Vannoy |
| 1,2 Chronicles | Raymond Dillard |
| Ezra | Edwin Yamauchi; Ronald Youngblood |
| Nehemiah | Edwin Yamauchi; Ronald Youngblood |
| Esther | Raymond Dillard; Edwin Yamauchi |
| Job | Elmer B. Smick; Ronald Youngblood |
| Psalms | John H. Stek |
| Proverbs | Herbert Wolf |
| Ecclesiastes | Derek Kidner |
| Song of Songs | John H. Stek |
| Isaiah | Herbert Wolf; John H. Stek |
| Jeremiah | Ronald Youngblood |
| Lamentations | Ronald Youngblood |
| Ezekiel | Mark Hillmer |
| Daniel | Gleason L. Archer, Jr.; Ronald Youngblood |
| Hosea | Jack P. Lewis |
| Joel | Jack P. Lewis |
| Amos | Alan R. Millard; John H. Stek |
| Obadiah | John M. Zinkand |
| Jonah | Marvin R. Wilson; John H. Stek |
| Micah | Allan A. MacRae; Thomas E. McComiskey |
| Nahum | G. Herbert Livingston; Kenneth L. Barker |
| Habakkuk | Roland K. Harrison; William C. Williams |
| Zephaniah | Roland K. Harrison |
| Haggai | Herbert Wolf |
| Zechariah | Kenneth L. Barker; Larry L. Walker |
| Malachi | Herbert Wolf; John H. Stek |
| Matthew | Ralph Earle |
| Mark | Walter W. Wessel; William L. Lane |
| Luke | Lewis Foster |
| John | Leon Morris |
| Acts | Lewis Foster |
| Romans | Walter W. Wessel |
| 1 Corinthians | W. Harold Mare |
| 2 Corinthians | Philip E. Hughes |
| Galatians | Robert Mounce |
| Ephesians | Walter L. Liefeld |
| Philippians | Richard B. Gaffin, Jr. |
| Colossians | Gerald F. Hawthorne; Wilber B. Wallis |
| 1,2 Thessalonians | Leon Morris |
| 1,2 Timothy | Walter W. Wessel; George W. Knight, III |
| Titus | D. Edmond Hiebert |
| Philemon | John Werner |
| Hebrews | Philip E. Hughes; Donald W. Burdick |
| James | Donald W. Burdick |
| 1,2 Peter | Donald W. Burdick; John H. Skilton |
| 1,2,3 John | Donald W. Burdick |
| Jude | Donald W. Burdick; John H. Skilton |
| Revelation | Robert Mounce |
| "The Time between the Testaments" (essay) | David O'Brien |

| | |
|---|---|
| Managing Editor: | Doris Wynbeek Rikkers |
| Copy Editor and Stylist: | June Gunden |
| Artist: | Hugh O. Claycombe |
| Art Consultant: | James E. Jennings |

# Gospel of John

# JOHN

See "The Synoptic Gospels," p. 1437.

## *Author*

The author is the apostle John, "the disciple whom Jesus loved" (13:23; 19:26; 20:2; 21:7,20,24). He was prominent in the early church but is not mentioned by name in this Gospel—which would be natural if he wrote it, but hard to explain otherwise. The author knew Jewish life well, as seen from references to popular Messianic speculations (e.g., 1:20-21; 7:40-42), to the hostility between Jews and Samaritans (4:9), and to Jewish customs, such as the duty of circumcision on the eighth day taking precedence over the prohibition of working on the Sabbath (see note on 7:22). He knew the geography of Palestine, locating Bethany about 15 stadia (about two miles) from Jerusalem (11:18) and mentioning Cana, a village not referred to in any earlier writing known to us (2:1; 21:2). The Gospel of John has many touches that were obviously based on the recollections of an eyewitness—such as the house at Bethany being filled with the fragrance of the broken perfume jar (12:3). Early writers such as Irenaeus and Tertullian say that John wrote this Gospel, and all other evidence agrees (see Introduction to 1 John: Author).

## *Date*

In general, two views of the dating of this Gospel have been advocated:

1. The traditional view places it toward the end of the first century, c. A.D. 85 or later (see Introduction to 1 John: Date).

2. More recently, some scholars have suggested an earlier date, perhaps as early as the 50s and no later than 70.

The first view may be supported by reference to the statement of Clement of Alexandria that John wrote to supplement the accounts found in the other Gospels (Eusebius, *Ecclesiastical History,* 6.14.7), and thus his Gospel is later than the first three. It has also been argued that the seemingly more developed theology of the fourth Gospel indicates that it originated later.

The second view has found favor because it has been felt more recently that John wrote independently of the other Gospels. This does not contradict the statement of Clement referred to above. Also, those who hold this view point out that developed theology does not necessarily argue for a late origin. The theology of Romans (written c. 57) is every bit as developed as that in John. Further, the statement in 5:2 that there "is" (rather than "was") a pool "near the Sheep Gate" may suggest a time before 70, when Jerusalem was destroyed. Others, however, observe that John elsewhere sometimes used the present tense when speaking of the past.

## *Purpose and Emphases*

Some interpreters have felt that John's aim was to set forth a version of the Christian message that would appeal to Greek thinkers. Others have seen a desire to supplement (or correct) the Synoptic Gospels, to combat some form of heresy, to oppose the continuing followers of John the Baptist or to achieve a similar goal. But the writer himself states his main purpose clearly: "These are written that you may believe that Jesus is the Christ, the Son of God, and that by believing you may have life in his name" (20:31). He may have had Greek readers mainly in mind, some of whom were being exposed to heretical influence, but his primary intention was evangelistic. It is possible to understand "may believe" in the sense of "may continue to believe"—in which case the purpose would be to build up believers as well as to win new converts.

For the main emphases of the book see notes on 1:4,7,9,14,19,49; 2:4,11; 3:27; 4:34; 6:35; 13:1-17:26; 13:31; 17:12,5; 20:31.

# INTRODUCTION: John

*Outline*

I. Prologue (1:1-18)
II. Beginnings of Jesus' Ministry (1:19-51)
  A. The Ministry of His Forerunner (1:19-34)
  B. Jesus' Introduction to Some Future Disciples (1:35-51)
III. Jesus' Public Ministry: Signs and Discourses (chs. 2-11)
  A. Changing Water to Wine (2:1-11)
  B. Cleansing the Temple (2:12-25)
  C. Interview with Nicodemus (3:1-21)
  D. Parallel Ministry with John the Baptist (3:22-4:3)
  E. Journey through Samaria: The Woman at the Well (4:4-42)
  F. Healing of the Official's Son (4:43-54)
  G. Trip to Jerusalem for an Annual Feast (ch. 5)
  H. The Feeding of the 5,000 and the Sermon on the Bread of Life (ch. 6)
  I. Jesus at the Feast of Tabernacles (chs. 7-8)
  J. Healing of the Man Born Blind (ch. 9)
  K. Parable of the Good Shepherd (10:1-21)
  L. Debating at the Feast of Dedication (10:22-39)
  M. Ministry in Perea (10:40-42)
  N. The Raising of Lazarus (ch. 11)
IV. The Passion Week (chs. 12-19)
  A. The Anointing of Jesus' Feet (12:1-11)
  B. The Triumphal Entry (12:12-19)
  C. The Coming of the Greeks (12:20-36)
  D. Continued Jewish Unbelief (12:37-50)
  E. Farewell Discourses (chs. 13-17)
    1. Discourse at the Last Supper (chs. 13-14)
    2. Discourse on the way to Gethsemane (chs. 15-16)
    3. Jesus' prayer of intercession (ch. 17)
  F. Jesus' Betrayal and Arrest (18:1-12)
  G. The Trials of Jesus (18:13-19:15)
  H. The Crucifixion and Burial (19:16-42)
V. The Resurrection (20:1-29)
VI. The Statement of Purpose (20:30-31)
VII. Epilogue (ch. 21)

## *The Word Became Flesh*

**1** In the beginning was the Word,[a] and
the Word was with God,[b] and the
Word was God.[c] 2He was with God in the
beginning.[d]
3Through him all things were made;
without him nothing was made that has
been made.[e] 4In him was life,[f] and that
life was the light[g] of men. 5The light
shines in the darkness,[h] but the darkness
has not understood**[a]** it.[i]
6There came a man who was sent from
God; his name was John.[j] 7He came as a
witness to testify[k] concerning that light, so
that through him all men might believe.[l]
8He himself was not the light; he came
only as a witness to the light. 9The true
light[m] that gives light to every man[n] was
coming into the world.**[b]**
10He was in the world, and though the
world was made through him,[o] the world
did not recognize him. 11He came to that
which was his own, but his own did not
receive him.[p] 12Yet to all who received
him, to those who believed[q] in his name,[r]
he gave the right to become children of
God[s]— 13children born not of natural de-
scent,**[c]** nor of human decision or a husband's will, but born of God.[t]
14The Word became flesh[u] and made
his dwelling among us. We have seen his
glory,[v] the glory of the One and Only,**[d]**
who came from the Father, full of grace[w]
and truth.[x]
15John testifies[y] concerning him. He
cries out, saying, "This was he of whom I
said, 'He who comes after me has sur-
passed me because he was before me.' "[z]
16From the fullness[a] of his grace[b] we have
all received one blessing after another.
17For the law was given through Moses;[c]
grace and truth came through Jesus
Christ.[d] 18No one has ever seen God,[e] but

**1:1** [a]Isa 55:11; Rev 19:13 [b]Jn 17:5; 1Jn 1:2 [c]Php 2:6 **1:2** [d]Ge 1:1; Jn 8:58; 17:5,24; 1Jn 1:1; Rev 1:8 **1:3** [e]ver 10; 1Co 8:6; Col 1:16; Heb 1:2 **1:4** [f]S Jn 5:26; 6:57; 11:25; 14:6; Ac 3:15; Heb 7:16; 1Jn 1:1,2; 5:20; Rev 1:18 [g]Ps 36:9; Jn 3:19; 8:12; 9:5; 12:46 **1:5** [h]Ps 18:28 [i]Jn 3:19 **1:6** [j]S Mt 3:1 **1:7** [k]ver 15,19, 32; Jn 3:26; 5:33 [l]ver 12; S Jn 3:15 **1:9** [m]1Jn 2:8 [n]Isa 49:6 **1:10** [o]S ver 3 **1:11** [p]Isa 53:3 **1:12** [q]ver 7; S Jn 3:15 [r]S 1Jn 3:23 [s]Dt 14:1; S Ro 8:14; 8:16, 21; Eph 5:1; 1Jn 3:1,2 **1:13** [t]Jn 3:6; Tit 3:5; Jas 1:18; 1Pe 1:23; 1Jn 3:9; 4:7; 5:1, 4

**1:14** [u]Gal 4:4; Php 2:7,8; 1Ti 3:16; Heb 2:14; 1Jn 1:1,2; 4:2 [v]Ex 33:18; 40:34 [w]S Ro 3:24 [x]Jn 14:6 **1:15** [y]ver 7 [z]ver 30; Mt 3:11 **1:16** [a]Eph 1:23; Col 1:19; 2:9 [b]S Ro 3:24 **1:17** [c]Dt 32:46; Jn 7:19 [d]ver 14 **1:18** [e]Ex 33:20; Jn 6:46; Col 1:15; 1Ti 6:16; 1Jn 4:12

**a** *5* Or *darkness, and the darkness has not overcome*
**b** *9* Or *This was the true light that gives light to every man who comes into the world*
**c** *13* Greek *of bloods*
**d** *14* Or *the Only Begotten*

**1:1** *In the beginning.* See Ge 1:1. *Word.* Greeks used this term not only of the spoken word but also of the unspoken word, the word still in the mind—the reason. When they applied it to the universe, they meant the rational principle that governs all things. Jews, on the other hand, used it as a way of referring to God. Thus John used a term that was meaningful to both Jews and Gentiles. *with God.* The Word was distinct from the Father. *was God.* Jesus was God in the fullest sense (see note on Ro 9:5). The prologue (vv. 1–18) begins and ends with a ringing affirmation of his deity (see note on v. 18).

**1:4** *life.* One of the great concepts of this Gospel. The term is found 36 times in John, while no other NT book uses it more than 17 times. Life is Christ's gift (10:28), and he, in fact, is "the life" (14:6). *light of men.* This Gospel also links light with Christ, from whom comes all spiritual illumination. He is the "light of the world," who holds out wonderful hope for man (8:12). For an OT link between life and light see Ps 36:9.

**1:5** *darkness.* The stark contrast between light and darkness is a striking theme in this Gospel (see, e.g., 12:35).

**1:6** *John.* In this Gospel the name John always refers to John the Baptist.

**1:7** *as a witness to testify.* John the Baptist's singular ministry was to testify to Jesus (10:41). "Witness" is another important concept in this Gospel. The noun ("witness" or "testimony") is used 14 times (in Matthew not at all, in Mark three times, in Luke once) and the verb ("testify") 33 times (found once each in Matthew and Luke, not at all in Mark)—in both cases more often than anywhere else in the NT. John (the author) thereby emphasizes that the facts about Jesus are amply attested. *that through him all men might believe.* People were not to believe "in" John the Baptist but "through" him. Similarly, the writer's purpose was to draw them to belief in Christ (20:31); he uses the verb "believe" 98 times.

**1:9** John is referring to the incarnation of Christ. *world.* Another common word in John's writings, found 78 times in this Gospel and 24 times in his letters (only 47 times in all of Paul's writings). It can mean the universe, the earth, the people on earth, most people, people opposed to God, or the human system opposed to God's purposes. John emphasizes the word by repetition, and moves without explanation from one meaning to another (see, e.g., 17:5,14–15 and notes).

**1:12** *he gave the right.* Membership in God's family is by grace alone—the gift of God (see Eph 2:8–9). It is never a human achievement, as v. 13 emphasizes; yet the imparting of the gift is dependent on man's reception of it, as the words "received" and "believed" make clear.

**1:14** *became.* Indicates transition; the Word existed before he became man. *flesh.* A strong, almost crude, word that stresses the reality of Christ's manhood. *made his dwelling among us. We have seen his glory.* The Greek for "made his dwelling" is connected with the word for "tent/tabernacle"; the verse would have reminded John's Jewish readers of the Tent of Meeting, which was filled by the glory of God (Ex 40:34–35). Christ revealed his glory to his disciples by the miracles he performed (see 2:11) and by his death and resurrection. *grace and truth.* The corresponding Hebrew terms are often translated "(unfailing) love and faithfulness" (see notes on Ps 26:3; Pr 16:6). *grace.* A significant Christian concept (see notes on Jnh 4:2; Gal 1:3; Eph 1:2), though John never uses the word after the prologue (vv. 1–18). *truth.* A word John uses 25 times and links closely with Jesus, who is the truth (14:6).

**1:15** *cries out.* The present tense indicates that John the Baptist's preaching still sounded in people's ears, though he was killed long before this Gospel was written. *he was before me.* In ancient times the older person was given respect and regarded as greater than the younger. People would normally have ranked Jesus lower in respect than John, who was older. John the Baptist explains that this is only apparent, since Jesus, as the Word, existed before he was born on earth.

**1:18** *God the One and Only.* An explicit declaration of Christ's deity (see vv. 1,14 and notes; 3:16). *has made him known.* Sometimes in the OT people are said to have seen God (e.g., Ex 24:9–11). But we are also told that no one can see God and live (Ex 33:20). Therefore, since no human

God the One and Only,[e,f] [f] who is at the
Father's side, has made him known.

### *John the Baptist Denies Being the Christ*

19 Now this was John's[g] testimony when
the Jews[h] of Jerusalem sent priests and Levites to ask him who he was. 20 He did not
fail to confess, but confessed freely, "I am
not the Christ.[g]" [i]
21 They asked him, "Then who are you?
Are you Elijah?" [j]
He said, "I am not."
"Are you the Prophet?" [k]
He answered, "No."
22 Finally they said, "Who are you? Give
us an answer to take back to those who
sent us. What do you say about yourself?"
23 John replied in the words of Isaiah the
prophet, "I am the voice of one calling in
the desert,[l] 'Make straight the way for the
Lord.' "[h] [m]
24 Now some Pharisees who had been
sent 25 questioned him, "Why then do you
baptize if you are not the Christ, nor Elijah,
nor the Prophet?"
26 "I baptize with[i] water,"[n] John replied, "but among you stands one you do
not know. 27 He is the one who comes after
me,[o] the thongs of whose sandals I am not
worthy to untie."[p]
28 This all happened at Bethany on the
other side of the Jordan,[q] where John was
baptizing.

### *Jesus the Lamb of God*

29 The next day John saw Jesus coming
toward him and said, "Look, the Lamb of
God,[r] who takes away the sin of the
world![s] 30 This is the one I meant when I
said, 'A man who comes after me has sur-
passed me because he was before me.'[t] 31 I
myself did not know him, but the reason I
came baptizing with water was that he
might be revealed to Israel."
32 Then John gave this testimony: "I saw
the Spirit come down from heaven as a
dove and remain on him.[u] 33 I would not
have known him, except that the one who

**1:18** [f]Jn 3:16,18; 1Jn 4:9
**1:19** [g]S Mt 3:1 [h]Jn 2:18; 5:10, 16; 6:41,52; 7:1; 10:24
**1:20** [i]Jn 3:28; Lk 3:15,16
**1:21** [j]S Mt 11:14 [k]Dt 18:15
**1:23** [l]Mt 3:1 [m]Isa 40:3
**1:26** [n]S Mk 1:4
**1:27** [o]ver 15,30 [p]Mk 1:7
**1:28** [q]Jn 3:26; 10:40
**1:29** [r]ver 36; Ge 22:8; Isa 53:7; 1Pe 1:19; Rev 5:6; 13:8 [s]S Jn 3:17
**1:30** [t]ver 15,27
**1:32** [u]Mt 3:16

[e] *18* Or *the Only Begotten* [f] *18* Some manuscripts *but the only* (or *only begotten*) *Son* [g] *20* Or *Messiah.* "The Christ" (Greek) and "the Messiah" (Hebrew) both mean "the Anointed One"; also in verse 25. [h] *23* Isaiah 40:3 [i] *26* Or *in*; also in verses 31 and 33

being can see God as he really is, those who saw God saw him in a form he took on himself temporarily for the occasion. Now, however, Christ has made him known.

**1:19** *the Jews.* The phrase occurs about 70 times in this Gospel. It is used in a favorable sense (e.g., 4:22) and in a neutral sense (e.g., 2:6). But generally John used it of the Jewish leaders who were hostile to Jesus (e.g., 8:48). Here it refers to the delegation sent by the Sanhedrin to look into the activities of an unauthorized teacher. *Levites.* Descendants of the tribe of Levi, who were assigned to specific duties in connection with the tabernacle and temple (Nu 3:17–37). They also had teaching responsibilities (2Ch 35:3; Ne 8:7–9), and it was probably in this role that they were sent with the priests to John the Baptist.

**1:20** *I.* Emphatic, contrasting John the Baptist (or Baptizer) with someone else. Throughout the following verses this emphatic "I" occurs frequently, and almost invariably there is an implied contrast with Jesus, who is always given the higher place.

**1:21** *Are you Elijah? . . . I am not.* The Jews remembered that Elijah had not died (2Ki 2:11) and believed that the same prophet would come back to earth to announce the end time. In this sense, John properly denied that he was Elijah. When Jesus later said the Baptist was Elijah (Mt 11:14; 17:10–13), he meant it in the sense that John was a fulfillment of the prophecy of Mal 4:5 (cf. Lk 1:17). *the Prophet.* The prophet of Dt 18:15,18. The Jewish people expected a variety of persons to be associated with the coming of the Messiah. John the Baptist emphatically denies being the Prophet. He had come to testify about Jesus, yet they kept asking him about himself. His answers became progressively more terse.

**1:23** The Baptist applied the prophecy of Isa 40:3 to his own ministry of calling people to repent in preparation for the coming of the Messiah. The men of Qumran (the community that produced the Dead Sea Scrolls; see "The Time between the Testaments," p. 1431) applied the same words to themselves, but they prepared for the Lord's coming by isolating themselves from the world to secure their own salvation. John concentrated on helping people come to the Messiah (the Christ).

**1:24** *Pharisees.* The conservative religious party, who probed deeper than the rest of the delegation (v. 19). See notes on Mt 3:7; Mk 2:16; Lk 5:17.

**1:25** *the Christ.* Means "the Anointed One" (see NIV text note on v. 20). In OT times anointing signified being set apart for service, particularly as king (cf. 1Sa 16:1,13; 26:11) or priest (Ex 40:13–15; Lev 4:3). But people were looking for not just *an* anointed one but *the* Anointed One, the Messiah.

**1:27** *whose sandals I am not worthy to untie.* A menial task, fit for a slave. Disciples would perform all sorts of service for their rabbis (teachers), but loosing sandal thongs was expressly excluded.

**1:28** *Bethany.* The Bethany mentioned elsewhere in the Gospels was only about two miles from Jerusalem. The site of this other Bethany is not known, except that it was located on the east side of the Jordan.

**1:29** *Lamb of God.* An expression found in the Bible only here and in v. 36. Many suggestions have been made as to its precise meaning (e.g., the lamb offered at Passover, or the lamb of Isa 53:7, of Jer 11:19 or of Ge 22:8). But the expression seems to be a general reference to sacrifice, not the name for a particular offering. John was saying that Jesus would be the sacrifice that would atone for the sin of the world.

**1:31** *I . . . did not know him.* John the Baptist, who "lived in the desert until he appeared publicly to Israel" (Lk 1:80), may not have known Jesus at all. But the words probably mean only that he did not know that Jesus was the Messiah until he saw the sign mentioned in vv. 32–33.

**1:32** See note on Mt 3:15 for Jesus' baptism.

**1:33** *he . . . will baptize with the Holy Spirit.* John baptized with water, but Jesus would baptize with the Spirit. If a specific event is intended by these words, the fulfillment was the sending of the Holy Spirit on the day of Pentecost (Ac 2).

sent me to baptize with water[v] told me,
'The man on whom you see the Spirit
come down and remain is he who will
baptize with the Holy Spirit.'[w] 34I have
seen and I testify that this is the Son of
God."[x]

### *Jesus' First Disciples*

*1:40–42pp — Mt 4:18–22; Mk 1:16–20; Lk 5:2–11*

35The next day John[y] was there again
with two of his disciples. 36When he saw
Jesus passing by, he said, "Look, the Lamb
of God!"[z]
37When the two disciples heard him say
this, they followed Jesus. 38Turning
around, Jesus saw them following and
asked, "What do you want?"
They said, "Rabbi"[a] (which means
Teacher), "where are you staying?"
39"Come," he replied, "and you will
see."
So they went and saw where he was
staying, and spent that day with him. It
was about the tenth hour.
40Andrew, Simon Peter's brother, was
one of the two who heard what John had
said and who had followed Jesus. 41The
first thing Andrew did was to find his
brother Simon and tell him, "We have
found the Messiah" (that is, the Christ).[b]
42And he brought him to Jesus.
Jesus looked at him and said, "You are
Simon son of John. You will be called[c]
Cephas" (which, when translated, is Peter[i]).[d]

### *Jesus Calls Philip and Nathanael*

43The next day Jesus decided to leave
for Galilee. Finding Philip,[e] he said to him,
"Follow me."[f]
44Philip, like Andrew and Peter, was
from the town of Bethsaida.[g] 45Philip
found Nathanael[h] and told him, "We have
found the one Moses wrote about in the
Law,[i] and about whom the prophets also
wrote[j]—Jesus of Nazareth,[k] the son of
Joseph."[l]
46"Nazareth! Can anything good come
from there?"[m] Nathanael asked.
"Come and see," said Philip.
47When Jesus saw Nathanael approaching, he said of him, "Here is a true Israelite,[n] in whom there is nothing false."[o]
48"How do you know me?" Nathanael
asked.
Jesus answered, "I saw you while you
were still under the fig tree before Philip
called you."
49Then Nathanael declared, "Rabbi,[p]
you are the Son of God;[q] you are the King
of Israel."[r]
50Jesus said, "You believe[k] because I
told you I saw you under the fig tree. You
shall see greater things than that." 51He
then added, "I tell you[l] the truth, you[l]
shall see heaven open,[s] and the angels of
God ascending and descending[t] on the
Son of Man."[u]

### *Jesus Changes Water to Wine*

2 On the third day a wedding took place
at Cana in Galilee.[v] Jesus' mother[w]
was there, 2and Jesus and his disciples had
also been invited to the wedding. 3When

[i]42 Both *Cephas* (Aramaic) and *Peter* (Greek) mean *rock.*
[k]50 Or *Do you believe . . . ?* [l]51 The Greek is plural.

**1:33** [v]S Mk 1:4
[w]S Mk 1:8
**1:34** [x]ver 49;
S Mt 4:3
**1:35** [y]S Mt 3:1
**1:36** [z]S ver 29
**1:38** [a]ver 49;
S Mt 23:7
**1:41** [b]Jn 4:25
**1:42** [c]Ge 17:5,
15; 32:28; 35:10
[d]Mt 16:18
**1:43** [e]Mt 10:3;
Jn 6:5-7; 12:21,
22; 14:8,9
[f]S Mt 4:19
**1:44** [g]S Mt 11:21
**1:45** [h]Jn 21:2
[i]S Lk 24:27
[j]S Lk 24:27
[k]S Mk 1:24
[l]Lk 3:23
**1:46** [m]Jn 7:41,
42,52
**1:47** [n]Ro 9:4,6
[o]Ps 32:2
**1:49** [p]ver 38;
S Mt 23:7 [q]ver
34; S Mt 4:3
[r]S Mt 2:2; 27:42;
Jn 12:13
**1:51** [s]S Mt 3:16
[t]Ge 28:12
[u]S Mt 8:20
**2:1** [v]Jn 4:46;
21:2 [w]S Mt 12:46

---

**1:34** *Son of God.* See vv. 14,18; 3:16; 20:31.
**1:35** *two.* One was Andrew (v. 40). The other is not named, but from early times it has been thought that he was the author of this Gospel. *his disciples.* In the sense that they had been baptized by John and looked to him as their religious teacher.
**1:36** *Lamb of God.* See note on v. 29.
**1:39** *tenth hour.* 4:00 P.M.
**1:41** *the Messiah.* See note on v. 25.
**1:42** *Peter.* See NIV text note. In the Gospels, Peter was anything but a rock; he was impulsive and unstable. In Acts, he was a pillar of the early church. Jesus named him not for what he was but for what, by God's grace, he would become.
**1:44** *Bethsaida.* See note on Mt 11:21.
**1:45** *son of Joseph.* Not a denial of the virgin birth of Christ (Mt 1:18,20,23,25; Lk 1:35). Joseph was Jesus' legal, though not his natural, father.
**1:46** *Nazareth.* See 7:52; see also note on Mt 2:23.
**1:47** *a true Israelite.* See 2:24–25.
**1:48** *fig tree.* Its shade was a favorite place for study and prayer in hot weather.
**1:49** *Son of God.* See vv. 14,18,34; 3:16; 20:31. At the beginning of Jesus' ministry Nathanael acknowledged Jesus with this meaningful title; later it was used in mockery (Mt 27:40; cf. Jn 19:7). *King of Israel.* See 12:13. In Mk 15:32 "Christ" and "King of Israel" are equated.
**1:51** *heaven open.* In Jesus' ministry the disciples will see heaven's (God's) testimony to Jesus as plainly as if they heard an announcement from heaven concerning him. *the angels of God ascending and descending.* As in Jacob's dream (see Ge 28:12 and note), thus marking Jesus as God's elect one through whom redemption comes to the world—perhaps identifying Jesus as *the* true Israelite (see v. 47). *Son of Man.* Jesus' favorite self-designation (see notes on Mk 8:31; Lk 6:5; 19:10).
**2:1** *a wedding.* Little is known of how a wedding was performed in first-century Palestine, but clearly the feast was very important and might go on for a week. To fail in proper hospitality was a serious offense. *Cana.* Mentioned only in John's Gospel (2:11; 4:46,50; 21:2). It was west of the Sea of Galilee, but the exact location is unknown.
**2:3** *When the wine was gone.* More than a minor social embarrassment, since the family had an obligation to provide a feast of the socially required standard. There was no great variety in beverages, and people normally drank water or wine.

## Miracles of Jesus

| Healing | MATTHEW | MARK | LUKE | JOHN |
|---|---|---|---|---|
| Man with leprosy | 8:2-4 | 1:40-42 | 5:12-13 | |
| Roman centurion's servant | 8:5-13 | | 7:1-10 | |
| Peter's mother-in-law | 8:14-15 | 1:30-31 | 4:38-39 | |
| Two men from Gadara | 8:28-34 | 5:1-15 | 8:27-35 | |
| Paralyzed man | 9:2-7 | 2:3-12 | 5:18-25 | |
| Woman with bleeding | 9:20-22 | 5:25-29 | 8:43-48 | |
| Two blind men | 9:27-31 | | | |
| Man mute and possessed | 9:32-33 | | | |
| Man with a shriveled hand | 12:10-13 | 3:1-5 | 6:6-10 | |
| Man blind, mute and possessed | 12:22 | | 11:14 | |
| Canaanite woman's daughter | 15:21-28 | 7:24-30 | | |
| Boy with a demon | 17:14-18 | 9:17-29 | 9:38-43 | |
| Two blind men (one named) | 20:29-34 | 10:46-52 | 18:35-43 | |
| Deaf mute | | 7:31-37 | | |
| Man possessed, synagogue | | 1:23-26 | 4:33-35 | |
| Blind man at Bethsaida | | 8:22-26 | | |
| Crippled woman | | | 13:11-13 | |
| Man with dropsy | | | 14:1-4 | |
| Ten men with leprosy | | | 17:11-19 | |
| The high priest's servant | | | 22:50-51 | |
| Official's son at Capernaum | | | | 4:46-54 |
| Sick man, pool of Bethesda | | | | 5:1-9 |
| Man born blind | | | | 9:1-7 |

| Command over the forces of nature | MATTHEW | MARK | LUKE | JOHN |
|---|---|---|---|---|
| Calming the storm | 8:23-27 | 4:37-41 | 8:22-25 | |
| Walking on the water | 14:25 | 6:48-51 | | 6:19-21 |
| 5,000 people fed | 14:15-21 | 6:35-44 | 9:12-17 | 6:5-13 |
| 4,000 people fed | 15:32-38 | 8:1-9 | | |
| Coin in the fish's mouth | 17:24-27 | | | |
| Fig tree withered | 21:18-22 | 11:12-14, 20-25 | | |
| Catch of fish | | | 5:4-11 | |
| Water turned into wine | | | | 2:1-11 |
| Another catch of fish | | | | 21:1-11 |

| Bringing the dead back to life | MATTHEW | MARK | LUKE | JOHN |
|---|---|---|---|---|
| Jairus's daughter | 9:18-19, 23-25 | 5:22-24, 38-42 | 8:41-42, 49-56 | |
| Widow's son at Nain | | | 7:11-15 | |
| Lazarus | | | | 11:1-44 |

the wine was gone, Jesus' mother said to
him, "They have no more wine."
4"Dear woman,[x] why do you involve
me?"[y] Jesus replied. "My time[z] has not yet
come."
5His mother said to the servants, "Do
whatever he tells you."[a]
6Nearby stood six stone water jars, the
kind used by the Jews for ceremonial
washing,[b] each holding from twenty to
thirty gallons.[m]
7Jesus said to the servants, "Fill the jars
with water"; so they filled them to the
brim.
8Then he told them, "Now draw some
out and take it to the master of the ban-
quet."
They did so, 9and the master of the ban-
quet tasted the water that had been turned
into wine.[c] He did not realize where it
had come from, though the servants who
had drawn the water knew. Then he called
the bridegroom aside 10and said, "Everyone brings out the choice wine first and
then the cheaper wine after the guests
have had too much to drink; but you have
saved the best till now."
11This, the first of his miraculous signs,[d]
Jesus performed at Cana in Galilee. He
thus revealed his glory,[e] and his disciples
put their faith in him.[f]

### Jesus Clears the Temple

*2:14-16pp — Mt 21:12,13; Mk 11:15-17; Lk 19:45,46*

12After this he went down to Capernaum[g] with his mother[h] and brothers[i]
and his disciples. There they stayed for a
few days.
13When it was almost time for the
Jewish Passover,[j] Jesus went up to Jerusalem.[k] 14In the temple courts he found men
selling cattle, sheep and doves,[l] and others sitting at tables exchanging money.[m]
15So he made a whip out of cords, and
drove all from the temple area, both sheep
and cattle; he scattered the coins of the
money changers and overturned their tables. 16To those who sold doves he said,
"Get these out of here! How dare you turn
my Father's house[n] into a market!"
17His disciples remembered that it is
written: "Zeal for your house will con-
sume me."[n] [o]
18Then the Jews[p] demanded of him,
"What miraculous sign[q] can you show us
to prove your authority to do all this?"[r]
19Jesus answered them, "Destroy this
temple, and I will raise it again in three
days."[s]
20The Jews replied, "It has taken forty-
six years to build this temple, and you are
going to raise it in three days?" 21But the
temple he had spoken of was his body.[t]
22After he was raised from the dead, his
disciples recalled what he had said.[u] Then
they believed the Scripture[v] and the
words that Jesus had spoken.
23Now while he was in Jerusalem at the
Passover Feast,[w] many people saw the miraculous signs[x] he was doing and be-

**2:4** [x]Jn 19:26 [y]S Mt 8:29 [z]S Mt 26:18
**2:5** [a]Ge 41:55
**2:6** [b]Mk 7:3,4; Jn 3:25
**2:9** [c]Jn 4:46
**2:11** [d]ver 23; Mt 12:38; Jn 3:2; S 4:48; 6:2,14,26, 30; 12:37; 20:30 [e]Jn 1:14 [f]Ex 14:31
**2:12** [g]S Mt 4:13 [h]S Mt 12:46 [i]S Mt 12:46
**2:13** [j]S Jn 11:55 [k]Dt 16:1-6; Lk 2:41
**2:14** [l]Lev 1:14; Dt 14:26 [m]Dt 14:25
**2:16** [n]Lk 2:49
**2:17** [o]Ps 69:9
**2:18** [p]S Jn 1:19 [q]S ver 11 [r]S Mt 12:38
**2:19** [s]S Mt 16:21; 26:61; 27:40; Mk 14:58; 15:29; Ac 6:14
**2:21** [t]1Co 6:19
**2:22** [u]Lk 24:5-8; Jn 12:16; 14:26 [v]Ps 16:10; S Lk 24:27
**2:23** [w]ver 13 [x]S ver 11

[m]6 Greek *two to three metretes* (probably about 75 to 115 liters) [n]17 Psalm 69:9

**2:4** *My time has not yet come.* Several similar expressions scattered through this Gospel (7:6,8,30; 8:20) picture Jesus moving inevitably toward the destiny for which he had come: the time of his sacrificial death on the cross. At the crucifixion and resurrection Jesus' time had truly come (12:23,27; 13:1; 16:32; 17:1).

**2:6** *ceremonial washing.* Jews became ceremonially defiled during the normal circumstances of daily life, and were cleansed by pouring water over the hands. For a lengthy feast with many guests a large amount of water was required for this purpose. *holding.* Refers to capacity, not actual content.

**2:11** *signs.* John always refers to Jesus' miracles as "signs," a word emphasizing the significance of the action rather than the marvel (see, e.g., 4:54; 6:14; 9:16; 11:47). They revealed Jesus' glory (see 1:14; cf. Isa 35:1–2; Joel 3:18; Am 9:13).

**2:12** *went down.* Situated on the shore of the lake, Capernaum was at a lower level than Cana. *brothers.* See note on Lk 8:19.

**2:13** *Passover.* See Ex 12 and notes on Ex 12:11–23; see also notes on Mt 26:17,18–30; Mk 14:1,12; Lk 22:1; and chart on "OT Feasts and Other Sacred Days," p. 176. Passover was one of the annual feasts that all Jewish men were required to celebrate in Jerusalem (Dt 16:16). See note on 5:1.

**2:14–17** Matthew, Mark and Luke record a cleansing of the temple toward the end of Jesus' ministry (see note on Mt 21:12–17).

**2:14** *cattle, sheep and doves.* Required for sacrifices. Jews who came great distances had to be able to buy sacrificial animals near the temple. The merchants, however, were selling them in the outer court of the temple itself, the one place where Gentiles could come to pray. *exchanging money.* Many coins had to be changed into currency acceptable to the temple authorities, which made money changers necessary (see note on Mk 11:15). They should not, however, have been working in the temple itself.

**2:19** The Jews thought Jesus was referring to the literal temple, but John tells us that he was not (v. 21). Years later Jesus was accused of saying that he would destroy the temple and raise it again (Mt 26:60–61; Mk 14:57–59), and mockers repeated the charge as he hung on the cross (Mt 27:40; Mk 15:29). The same misunderstanding may have been behind the charge against Stephen (Ac 6:14).

**2:20** *forty-six years.* The temple was not finally completed until A.D. 64. The meaning is that work had been going on for 46 years. Since it had begun in 20 B.C., the year of the event recorded here is A.D. 26.

**2:22** *recalled.* See 14:26.

**2:23** *the Passover Feast.* See note on v. 13. *name.* In ancient times an individual's "name" summed up his whole person (see NIV text note).

lieved[y] in his name.[o] 24But Jesus would
not entrust himself to them, for he knew
all men. 25He did not need man's testimony about man,[z] for he knew what was
in a man.[a]

## *Jesus Teaches Nicodemus*

3 Now there was a man of the Pharisees
named Nicodemus,[b] a member of the
Jewish ruling council.[c] 2He came to Jesus
at night and said, "Rabbi,[d] we know[e] you
are a teacher who has come from God. For
no one could perform the miraculous
signs[f] you are doing if God were not with
him."[g]
3In reply Jesus declared, "I tell you the
truth, no one can see the kingdom of God
unless he is born again.[p]"[h] [i]
4"How can a man be born when he is
old?" Nicodemus asked. "Surely he cannot
enter a second time into his mother's
womb to be born!"
5Jesus answered, "I tell you the truth,
no one can enter the kingdom of God unless he is born of water and the Spirit.[j] [k]
6Flesh gives birth to flesh, but the Spirit[q]
gives birth to spirit.[l] 7You should not be
surprised at my saying, 'You[r] must be
born again.' 8The wind blows wherever it
pleases. You hear its sound, but you cannot
tell where it comes from or where it is
going. So it is with everyone born of the
Spirit."[m]
9"How can this be?"[n] Nicodemus
asked.
10"You are Israel's teacher,"[o] said Jesus,
"and do you not understand these things?
11I tell you the truth, we speak of what we
know,[p] and we testify to what we have
seen, but still you people do not accept our
testimony.[q] 12I have spoken to you of
earthly things and you do not believe; how
then will you believe if I speak of heavenly
things? 13No one has ever gone into
heaven[r] except the one who came from
heaven[s]—the Son of Man.[s] [t] 14Just as
Moses lifted up the snake in the desert,[u]
so the Son of Man must be lifted up,[v]
15that everyone who believes[w] in him may
have eternal life.[t] [x]
16"For God so loved[y] the world that he
gave[z] his one and only Son,[u] [a] that whoever believes[b] in him shall not perish but
have eternal life.[c] 17For God did not send
his Son into the world[d] to condemn the
world, but to save the world through
him.[e] 18Whoever believes in him is not
condemned,[f] but whoever does not believe stands condemned already because
he has not believed in the name of God's
one and only Son.[v] [g] 19This is the verdict:
Light[h] has come into the world, but men
loved darkness instead of light because
their deeds were evil.[i] 20Everyone who
does evil hates the light, and will not come
into the light for fear that his deeds will be
exposed.[j] 21But whoever lives by the
truth comes into the light, so that it may be
seen plainly that what he has done has
been done through God."[w]

## *John the Baptist's Testimony About Jesus*

22After this, Jesus and his disciples went

**2:23** [y]S Jn 3:15 **2:25** [z]Isa 11:3 [a]Dt 31:21; 1Ki 8:39; S Mt 9:4; Jn 6:61, 64; 13:11 **3:1** [b]Jn 7:50; 19:39 [c]Lk 23:13 **3:2** [d]S Mt 23:7 [e]ver 11 [f]S Jn 2:11 [g]Jn 10:38; 14:10, 11; Ac 2:22; 10:38 **3:3** [h]S Jn 1:13 [i]S Mt 3:2 **3:5** [j]S Ac 22:16 [k]Tit 3:5 **3:6** [l]S Jn 1:13; 1Co 15:50 **3:8** [m]1Co 2:14-16 **3:9** [n]Jn 6:52,60 **3:10** [o]Lk 2:46 **3:11** [p]Jn 1:18; 7:16,17 [q]ver 32 **3:13** [r]Pr 30:4; Ac 2:34; Eph 4:8-10 [s]ver 31; Jn 6:38,42; Heb 4:14; 9:24 [t]S Mt 8:20 **3:14** [u]Nu 21:8,9 [v]S Jn 12:32 **3:15** [w]ver 16,36; Ge 15:6; Nu 14:11; Mt 27:42; Mk 1:15; Jn 1:7, 12; 2:23; 5:24; 7:38; 20:29; Ac 13:39; 16:31; Ro 3:22; 10:9,10; 1Jn 5:1,5,10 [x]ver 16,36; S Mt 25:46; Jn 20:31 **3:16** [y]Ro 5:8; Eph 2:4; 1Jn 4:9, 10 [z]Isa 9:6; Ro 8:32 [a]Ge 22:12; Jn 1:18 [b]S ver 15 [c]ver 36; Jn 6:29, 40; 11:25,26 **3:17** [d]Jn 6:29,57; 10:36; 11:42; 17:8,21; 20:21 [e]Isa 53:11; S Mt 1:21; S Lk 2:11; 19:10; Jn 1:29; 12:47; S Ro 11:14; 1Ti 1:15; 2:5,6; 1Jn 2:2; 3:5

**3:18** [f]Jn 5:24 [g]Jn 1:18; 1Jn 4:9 **3:19** [h]S Jn 1:4 [i]Ps 52:3; Jn 7:7 **3:20** [j]Eph 5:11,13

[o]*23* Or *and believed in him* [p]*3* Or *born from above*; also in verse 7 [q]*6* Or *but spirit* [r]*7* The Greek is plural. [s]*13* Some manuscripts *Man, who is in heaven* [t]*15* Or *believes may have eternal life in him* [u]*16* Or *his only begotten Son* [v]*18* Or *God's only begotten Son* [w]*21* Some interpreters end the quotation after verse 15.

---

**3:1** *a man of the Pharisees.* See notes on Mt 3:7; Mk 2:16; Lk 5:17.

**3:2** *at night.* Perhaps Nicodemus was afraid to come by day. Or he may have wanted a long talk, which would have been difficult in the daytime with the crowds around Jesus.

**3:3** *born again.* The Greek also may mean "born from above" (see NIV text note). Both meanings are consistent with Jesus' redeeming work.

**3:5** *kingdom of God.* See note on Mt 3:2. *born of water and the Spirit.* A phrase understood in various ways: 1. It means much the same as "born of the Spirit" (v. 8; cf. Tit 3:5). 2. Water here refers to purification. 3. Water refers to baptism—that of John (1:31) or that of Jesus and his disciples (v. 22; 4:1–2).

**3:7** *You.* See NIV text note. This assertion applies to everyone, not just Nicodemus. *must.* There are no exceptions. *born again.* See note on v. 3.

**3:8** The Holy Spirit is sovereign. He works as he pleases in his renewal of the human heart.

**3:11** *we.* The plural associates others, perhaps the disciples, with Jesus. The words are true of Christians as well as of Christ. *testimony.* See note on 1:7.

**3:13** *the Son of Man.* Jesus' favorite self-designation (see notes on Mk 8:31; Lk 6:5; 19:10).

**3:14** *the Son of Man must be lifted up.* See notes on 12:31–32.

**3:15** *believes.* See note on 1:7. *eternal life.* An infinitely high quality of life in living fellowship with God—both now and forever.

**3:16** *God so loved the world.* The great truth that motivated God's plan of salvation (cf. 1Jn 4:9–10). *world.* All people on earth—or perhaps all creation (see note on 1:9). *that he gave.* See Isa 9:6. *one and only Son.* See 1:14,18; cf. Ge 22:2,16; Ro 8:32. Although believers are also called "sons of God" (2Co 6:18; Rev 21:7), Jesus is uniquely God's Son.

**3:18** *believes . . . does not believe.* John is not speaking of momentary beliefs and doubts but of continuing, settled attitudes.

**3:22** *baptized.* According to 4:2 only the disciples actually baptized.

out into the Judean countryside, where he
spent some time with them, and baptized.[k] 23Now John[l] also was baptizing at
Aenon near Salim, because there was
plenty of water, and people were con-
stantly coming to be baptized. 24(This was
before John was put in prison.)[m] 25An argument developed between some of John's
disciples and a certain Jew[x] over the matter of ceremonial washing.[n] 26They came
to John and said to him, "Rabbi,[o] that man
who was with you on the other side of the
Jordan—the one you testified[p] about
—well, he is baptizing, and everyone
is going to him."

27To this John replied, "A man can receive only what is given him from heaven.
28You yourselves can testify that I said, 'I
am not the Christ[y] but am sent ahead of
him.'[q] 29The bride belongs to the bridegroom.[r] The friend who attends the bridegroom waits and listens for him, and is full
of joy when he hears the bridegroom's
voice. That joy is mine, and it is now complete.[s] 30He must become greater; I must
become less.

31"The one who comes from above[t] is
above all; the one who is from the earth
belongs to the earth, and speaks as one
from the earth.[u] The one who comes from
heaven is above all. 32He testifies to what
he has seen and heard,[v] but no one accepts his testimony.[w] 33The man who has
accepted it has certified that God is truthful. 34For the one whom God has sent[x]
speaks the words of God, for God[z] gives
the Spirit[y] without limit. 35The Father
loves the Son and has placed everything in
his hands.[z] 36Whoever believes in the Son
has eternal life,[a] but whoever rejects the
Son will not see life, for God's wrath remains on him."[a]

**3:22** [k]Jn 4:2
**3:23** [l]S Mt 3:1
**3:24** [m]Mt 4:12; 14:3
**3:25** [n]Jn 2:6
**3:26** [o]S Mt 23:7 [p]Jn 1:7
**3:28** [q]Jn 1:20,23
**3:29** [r]Mt 9:15 [s]Jn 16:24; 17:13; Php 2:2; 1Jn 1:4; 2Jn 12
**3:31** [t]ver 13 [u]Jn 8:23; 1Jn 4:5
**3:32** [v]Jn 8:26; 15:15 [w]ver 11
**3:34** [x]S ver 17 [y]Isa 42:1; Mt 12:18; Lk 4:18; Ac 10:38
**3:35** [z]S Mt 28:18
**3:36** [a]S ver 15; Jn 5:24; 6:47
**4:1** [b]Jn 3:22,26
**4:3** [c]S Lk 7:13 [d]Jn 3:22
**4:4** [e]S Mt 10:5
**4:5** [f]Ge 33:19; Jos 24:32

### *Jesus Talks With a Samaritan Woman*

4 The Pharisees heard that Jesus was
gaining and baptizing more disciples
than John,[b] 2although in fact it was not
Jesus who baptized, but his disciples.
3When the Lord[c] learned of this, he left
Judea[d] and went back once more to Galilee.

4Now he had to go through Samaria.[e]
5So he came to a town in Samaria called
Sychar, near the plot of ground Jacob had
given to his son Joseph.[f] 6Jacob's well was
there, and Jesus, tired as he was from the
journey, sat down by the well. It was about
the sixth hour.

7When a Samaritan woman came to

[x]*25* Some manuscripts *and certain Jews* [y]*28* Or *Messiah* [z]*34* Greek *he* [a]*36* Some interpreters end the quotation after verse 30.

**3:23** *Aenon.* Possibly about eight miles south of Scythopolis (Beth Shan), west of the Jordan.
**3:25** *argument . . . over . . . ceremonial washing.* The Dead Sea (Qumran) Scrolls (see "The Time between the Testaments," p. 1431) show that some Jews were deeply interested in the right way to achieve ceremonial purification.
**3:26** *testified.* See note on 1:7. John's disciples knew that he had testified about Jesus, but they loved their master and were envious of Jesus' success.
**3:27** The words are true of both Jesus and John (and of everyone). Both had what God had given them, so there was no place for envy. *given.* The verb "to give" is used frequently in this Gospel (76 times), especially of the things the Father gives the Son.
**3:29** *the bridegroom.* The most important man at a wedding, referring here to Jesus. The friend (best man) is there only to help the bridegroom, which describes the role of John the Baptist. *full of joy.* Not because he was on center stage, but because the bridegroom was there. John's joy was to hear of Jesus' success.
**3:30** John the Baptist had been sent to prepare the way for the Messiah and here reaffirms his subordinate position.
**3:31** *The one who comes from above.* Jesus, whose heavenly origin (cf. 1Co 15:47) meant much to John. *the one who is from the earth.* A general expression that could apply to anyone, but here it particularly refers to John the Baptist.
**3:32** *what he has seen and heard.* Jesus taught from divine experience. *no one.* Does not mean that no person accepted what he said (see v. 33) but that people in general refused his teaching.
**3:33** *certified.* When anyone accepts Christ's testimony, he accepts the truth that Jesus came from heaven and that God was acting in him for the world's salvation. He thereby certifies that God is truthful.
**3:34** *the one whom God has sent.* Jesus. *without limit.* Some hold that it is only to Jesus that the Spirit is given without limit. Others take the "he" (see NIV text note) as a reference to Christ's giving the Spirit without limit to believers.
**3:36** *has.* Eternal life is a present possession, not something the believer will only obtain later (see note on v. 15). *God's wrath.* A strong expression, meaning that God is actively opposed to everything evil. The word "wrath" occurs only here in John's Gospel (see note on Ro 1:18). *remains.* A sinner cannot expect God's wrath eventually to fade away. God's opposition to evil is both total and permanent.
**4:1** *Pharisees.* The religious leaders took a close interest in John the Baptist (see note on 1:24) and then also in Jesus.
**4:2** The disciples did not baptize without Jesus' approval (3:22).
**4:3** *left Judea.* Success (which aroused opposition; see 7:1), not failure, led Jesus to leave Judea.
**4:4** *had to go.* The necessity lay in Jesus' mission, not in geography. *Samaria.* Here the whole region, not simply the city. Jews often avoided Samaria by crossing the Jordan and traveling on the east side (see notes on Mt 10:5; Lk 9:52).
**4:5** *Sychar.* A small village near Shechem. Jacob bought some land in the vicinity of Shechem (Ge 33:18–19), and it was apparently this land that he gave to Joseph (Ge 48:21–22).
**4:6** *Jacob's well.* Mentioned nowhere else in Scripture. *about the sixth hour.* About 12:00 noon.
**4:7** *to draw water.* People normally drew water at the end of the day rather than in the heat of midday (see Ge 24:11 and note). But the practice is attested by Josephus, who says

draw water, Jesus said to her, "Will you
give me a drink?"[g] 8(His disciples had
gone into the town[h] to buy food.)
9The Samaritan woman said to him,
"You are a Jew and I am a Samaritan[i]
woman. How can you ask me for a drink?"
(For Jews do not associate with Samaritans.[b])
10Jesus answered her, "If you knew the
gift of God and who it is that asks you for a
drink, you would have asked him and he
would have given you living water."[j]
11"Sir," the woman said, "you have
nothing to draw with and the well is deep.
Where can you get this living water? 12Are
you greater than our father Jacob, who
gave us the well[k] and drank from it himself, as did also his sons and his flocks and
herds?"
13Jesus answered, "Everyone who
drinks this water will be thirsty again,
14but whoever drinks the water I give him
will never thirst.[l] Indeed, the water I give
him will become in him a spring of water[m]
welling up to eternal life."[n]
15The woman said to him, "Sir, give me
this water so that I won't get thirsty[o] and
have to keep coming here to draw water."
16He told her, "Go, call your husband
and come back."
17"I have no husband," she replied.
Jesus said to her, "You are right when
you say you have no husband. 18The fact
is, you have had five husbands, and the
man you now have is not your husband.
What you have just said is quite true."
19"Sir," the woman said, "I can see that
you are a prophet.[p] 20Our fathers worshiped on this mountain,[q] but you Jews
claim that the place where we must worship is in Jerusalem."[r]
21Jesus declared, "Believe me, woman,
a time is coming[s] when you will worship
the Father neither on this mountain nor in
Jerusalem.[t] 22You Samaritans worship
what you do not know;[u] we worship what
we do know, for salvation is from the
Jews.[v] 23Yet a time is coming and has now
come[w] when the true worshipers will worship the Father in spirit[x] and truth, for
they are the kind of worshipers the Father
seeks. 24God is spirit,[y] and his worshipers
must worship in spirit and in truth."
25The woman said, "I know that Messiah" (called Christ)[z] "is coming. When
he comes, he will explain everything to
us."
26Then Jesus declared, "I who speak to
you am he."[a]

**4:7** [g]Ge 24:17; 1Ki 17:10
**4:8** [h]ver 5,39
**4:9** [i]S Mt 10:5
**4:10** [j]Isa 44:3; 55:1; Jer 2:13; 17:13; Zec 14:8; Jn 7:37,38; Rev 7:17; 21:6; 22:1,17
**4:12** [k]ver 6
**4:14** [l]Jn 6:35 [m]Isa 12:3; 58:11; Jn 7:38 [n]S Mt 25:46
**4:15** [o]Jn 6:34
**4:19** [p]S Mt 21:11
**4:20** [q]Dt 11:29; Jos 8:33 [r]Lk 9:53
**4:21** [s]Jn 5:28; 16:2 [t]Mal 1:11; 1Ti 2:8
**4:22** [u]2Ki 17:28-41 [v]Isa 2:3; Ro 3:1,2; 9:4,5; 15:8,9
**4:23** [w]Jn 5:25; 16:32 [x]Php 3:3
**4:24** [y]Php 3:3
**4:25** [z]Mt 1:16; Jn 1:41
**4:26** [a]Jn 8:24; 9:35-37

[b]9 Or *do not use dishes Samaritans have used*

that the young ladies whom Moses helped (Ex 2:15–17) came to draw water at noon.

**4:9** The point of the NIV text note (and probably of the text) is that a Jew would become ceremonially unclean if he used a drinking vessel handled by a Samaritan, since the Jews held that all Samaritans were "unclean."

**4:10** *gift.* The Greek for this word is used only here in this Gospel and emphasizes God's grace through Christ. Jesus gave life and gave it freely. *living water.* In 7:38–39 the term is explained as meaning the Holy Spirit, but here it refers to eternal life (see v. 14).

**4:11** *deep.* Christian pilgrim sources as early as the fourth century mention a well in this area that was about 100 feet deep. When the present well was cleaned out in 1935, it was found to be 138 feet deep.

**4:12** *our father Jacob.* Respect for the past prevented her from seeing the great opportunity of the present.

**4:14** *welling up.* The expression is a vigorous one, with a meaning like "leaping up." Jesus was speaking of vigorous, abundant life (cf. 10:10).

**4:15** Cf. the misunderstanding of Nicodemus (3:4). In both cases the way was opened for further instruction.

**4:18** *five husbands.* The Jews held that a woman might be divorced twice or at the most three times. If the Samaritans had the same standard, the woman's life had been exceedingly immoral. Apparently she had not married her present partner.

**4:19** *a prophet.* Because of his special insight.

**4:20** *this mountain.* Perhaps the woman did not like the way the conversation was going and so began to argue. The proper place of worship had long been a source of debate between Jews and Samaritans. Samaritans held that "this mountain" (Mount Gerizim) was especially sacred. Abraham and Jacob had built altars in the general vicinity (Ge 12:7; 33:20), and the people had been blessed from this mountain (Dt 11:29; 27:12). In the Samaritan Scriptures, Mount Gerizim (rather than Mount Ebal) was the mountain on which Moses had commanded an altar to be built (Dt 27:4–6). The Samaritans had built a temple on Mount Gerizim c. 400 B.C., which the Jews destroyed c. 128. Both actions, of course, increased hostility between the two groups.

**4:22** *worship what you do not know.* The Samaritan Bible contained only the Pentateuch. They worshiped the true God, but their failure to accept much of his revelation meant that they knew little of him. *salvation is from the Jews.* The Messiah would be a Jew.

**4:24** *God is spirit . . . worship in spirit and in truth.* The place of worship is irrelevant, because true worship must be in keeping with God's nature, which is spirit. In John's Gospel truth is associated with Christ (14:6; see note on 1:14), a fact that has great importance for the proper understanding of Christian worship.

**4:25** *Messiah . . . will explain everything.* The woman's last attempt to evade the issue. The matter was too important, she reasoned, for people like Jesus and herself to work out. Understanding would have to await the coming of the Messiah (see note on 1:25). The Samaritans expected a Messiah, but their rejection of all the inspired writings after the Pentateuch meant that they knew little about him. They thought of him mainly as a teacher.

**4:26** *I . . . am he.* The only occasion before his trial on which Jesus specifically said that he was the Messiah (but see Mk 9:41). The term did not have the political overtones in Samaria that it had in Judea, which may be part of the reason Jesus used the designation here.

# Jesus in Judea and Samaria

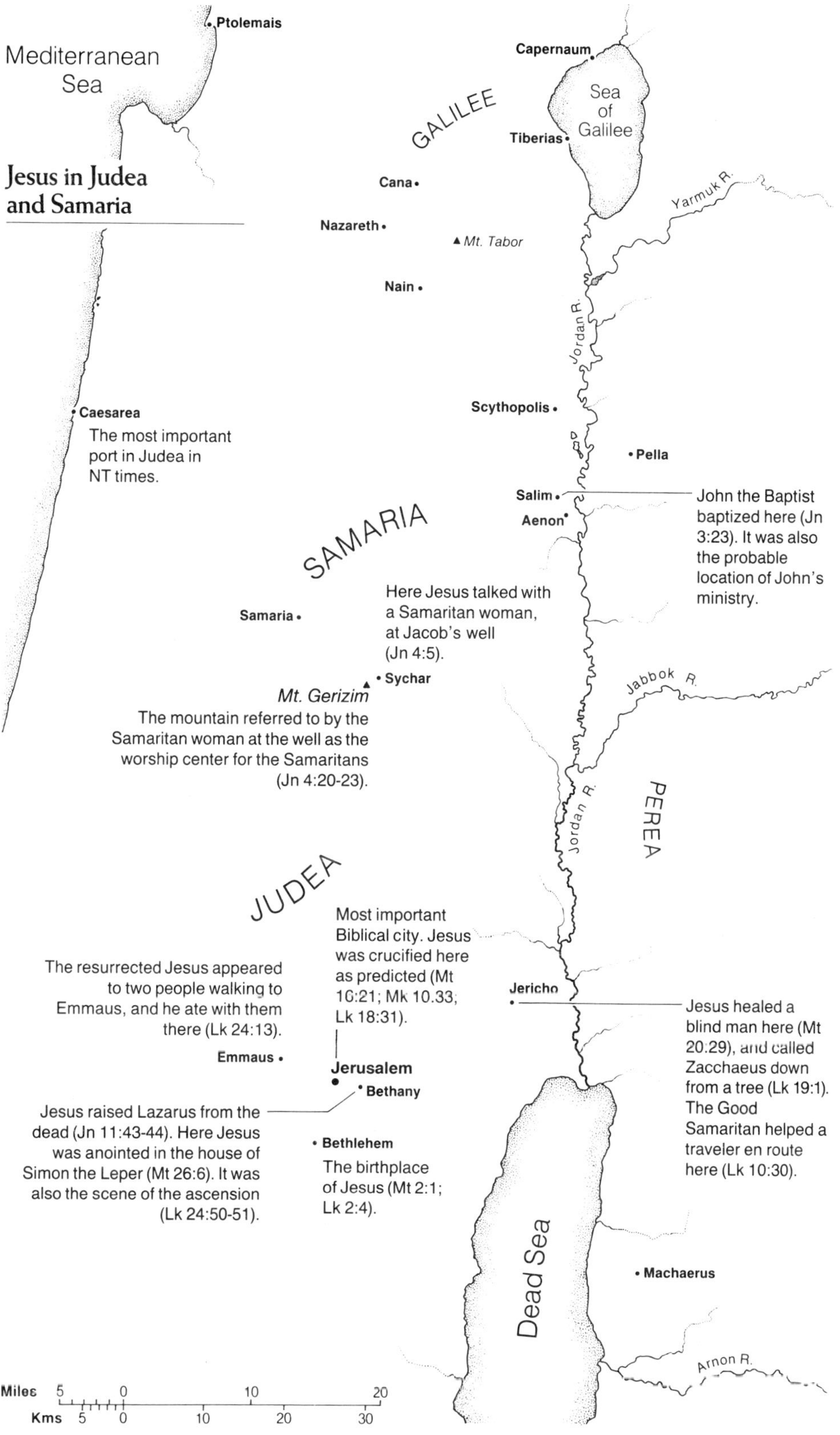

### The Disciples Rejoin Jesus

27Just then his disciples returned[b] and
were surprised to find him talking with a
woman. But no one asked, "What do you
want?" or "Why are you talking with
her?"
28Then, leaving her water jar, the
woman went back to the town and said to
the people, 29"Come, see a man who told
me everything I ever did.[c] Could this be
the Christ[c]?"[d] 30They came out of the
town and made their way toward him.
31Meanwhile his disciples urged him,
"Rabbi,[e] eat something."
32But he said to them, "I have food to
eat[f] that you know nothing about."
33Then his disciples said to each other,
"Could someone have brought him food?"
34"My food," said Jesus, "is to do the
will[g] of him who sent me and to finish his
work.[h] 35Do you not say, 'Four months
more and then the harvest'? I tell you,
open your eyes and look at the fields! They
are ripe for harvest.[i] 36Even now the reaper draws his wages, even now he har-
vests[j] the crop for eternal life,[k] so that the
sower and the reaper may be glad together. 37Thus the saying 'One sows and
another reaps'[l] is true. 38I sent you to reap
what you have not worked for. Others
have done the hard work, and you have
reaped the benefits of their labor."

### Many Samaritans Believe

39Many of the Samaritans from that
town[m] believed in him because of the
woman's testimony, "He told me everything I ever did."[n] 40So when the Samaritans came to him, they urged him to stay
with them, and he stayed two days. 41And
because of his words many more became
believers.
42They said to the woman, "We no
longer believe just because of what you
said; now we have heard for ourselves,
and we know that this man really is the
Savior of the world."[o]

### Jesus Heals the Official's Son

43After the two days[p] he left for Galilee.
44(Now Jesus himself had pointed out that
a prophet has no honor in his own country.)[q] 45When he arrived in Galilee, the
Galileans welcomed him. They had seen
all that he had done in Jerusalem at the
Passover Feast,[r] for they also had been
there.
46Once more he visited Cana in Galilee,
where he had turned the water into
wine.[s] And there was a certain royal official whose son lay sick at Capernaum.
47When this man heard that Jesus had arrived in Galilee from Judea,[t] he went to
him and begged him to come and heal his
son, who was close to death.
48"Unless you people see miraculous
signs and wonders," Jesus told him, "you
will never believe."[u]
49The royal official said, "Sir, come
down before my child dies."
50Jesus replied, "You may go. Your son
will live."
The man took Jesus at his word and de-
parted. 51While he was still on the way, his
servants met him with the news that his

**4:27** [b]ver 8 **4:29** [c]ver 17,18 [d]Mt 12:23; Jn 7:26,31 **4:31** [e]S Mt 23:7 **4:32** [f]Job 23:12; Mt 4:4; Jn 6:27 **4:34** [g]S Mt 26:39 [h]S Jn 19:30 **4:35** [i]Mt 9:37; Lk 10:2 **4:36** [j]Ro 1:13 [k]S Mt 25:46 **4:37** [l]Job 31:8; Mic 6:15 **4:39** [m]ver 5 [n]ver 29

**4:42** [o]S Lk 2:11 **4:43** [p]ver 40 **4:44** [q]Mt 13:57; Lk 4:24 **4:45** [r]Jn 2:23 **4:46** [s]Jn 2:1-11 **4:47** [t]ver 3,54 **4:48** [u]Da 4:2,3; S Jn 2:11; Ac 2:43; 14:3; Ro 15:19; 2Co 12:12; Heb 2:4

[c]29 Or *Messiah*

---

**4:27** *were surprised.* Jewish religious teachers rarely spoke with women in public.
**4:29** *everything I ever did.* An exaggeration, but it shows the impression Jesus made on her. *Could this be the Christ?* Her question seems full of longing, as though she did not expect them to say "Yes," but she could not say "No."
**4:33** A misunderstanding similar to that of the woman (v. 15).
**4:34** *My food . . . is to do the will of him who sent me.* John often mentions that Jesus depended on the Father and did the work the Father sent him to do (e.g., 5:30; 6:38; 8:26; 9:4; 10:37–38; 12:49–50; 14:31; 15:10; 17:4).
**4:35** *Four months more and then the harvest.* Apparently a proverb that meant something like "Harvest cannot be rushed." But, while the crops must take their time ripening, in the fields that Jesus referred to the harvest is already ripe.
**4:36** *draws his wages.* The work, or at least part of it, had been done, and others were working hard. The disciples were not to think that the harvest was far off. Jesus was not speaking of grain but of "the crop for eternal life." There was urgency, for the crop would not wait. *glad together.* There is no competition among Christ's faithful servants, and sower and reaper share in the joy of the crop.
**4:37** See 1Co 3:6–9.
**4:38** *Others.* May refer to John the Baptist and his supporters, on whose work the apostles would build. Or perhaps Jesus was looking further back, to the prophets and other godly men of old. Either way, he expected the apostles to be reapers as well as sowers.
**4:42** *the Savior of the world.* In the NT the expression occurs only here and in 1Jn 4:14. It points to the facts (1) that Jesus not only teaches but also saves, and (2) that his salvation extends to the world (see note on 3:16).
**4:44** *a prophet has no honor in his own country.* Nonetheless, Jesus went to Galilee, because he came to die for our salvation (cf. 1:29).
**4:45** *welcomed him.* The welcome of the Galileans actually was a kind of rejection, for they were interested only in his miracles. They were not welcoming the Messiah who could save them, but only a miracle worker who could amaze them.
**4:46** *royal official.* Evidently an officer in Herod's service.
**4:48** *Unless you . . . see . . . signs and wonders . . . you will never believe.* The general attitude of Galileans, not that of the official.
**4:50** *Your son will live.* Not simply a prophecy, but words of power. Jesus was healing, not forecasting a happy ending (see vv. 51,53).

boy was living. 52When he inquired as to
the time when his son got better, they said
to him, "The fever left him yesterday at
the seventh hour."
53Then the father realized that this was
the exact time at which Jesus had said to
him, "Your son will live." So he and all his
household[v] believed.
54This was the second miraculous sign[w]
that Jesus performed, having come from
Judea to Galilee.

## *The Healing at the Pool*

5 Some time later, Jesus went up to
Jerusalem for a feast of the Jews. 2Now
there is in Jerusalem near the Sheep Gate[x]
a pool, which in Aramaic[y] is called Bethesda[d] and which is surrounded by five
covered colonnades. 3Here a great number
of disabled people used to lie—the blind,
the lame, the paralyzed.[e] 5One who was
there had been an invalid for thirty-eight
years. 6When Jesus saw him lying there
and learned that he had been in this condition for a long time, he asked him, "Do
you want to get well?"
7"Sir," the invalid replied, "I have no
one to help me into the pool when the
water is stirred. While I am trying to get in,
someone else goes down ahead of me."
8Then Jesus said to him, "Get up! Pick
up your mat and walk."[z] 9At once the
man was cured; he picked up his mat and
walked.
The day on which this took place was a
Sabbath,[a] 10and so the Jews[b] said to the
man who had been healed, "It is the Sabbath; the law forbids you to carry your
mat."[c]
11But he replied, "The man who made
me well said to me, 'Pick up your mat and
walk.' "
12So they asked him, "Who is this fellow
who told you to pick it up and walk?"
13The man who was healed had no idea
who it was, for Jesus had slipped away into
the crowd that was there.
14Later Jesus found him at the temple
and said to him, "See, you are well again.
Stop sinning[d] or something worse may
happen to you." 15The man went away
and told the Jews[e] that it was Jesus who
had made him well.

## *Life Through the Son*

16So, because Jesus was doing these
things on the Sabbath, the Jews persecuted
him. 17Jesus said to them, "My Father[f] is

**4:53** [v]S Ac 11:14 **4:54** [w]S ver 48; S Jn 2:11 **5:2** [x]Ne 3:1; 12:39 [y]Jn 19:13, 17,20; 20:16; Ac 21:40; 22:2; 26:14 **5:8** [z]Mt 9:5,6 **5:9** [a]Mt 12:1-14; Jn 9:14 **5:10** [b]ver 16 [c]Ne 13:15-22; Jer 17:21; S Mt 12:2 **5:14** [d]Mk 2:5; Jn 8:11 **5:15** [e]S Jn 1:19 **5:17** [f]Lk 2:49

[d] *2* Some manuscripts *Bethzatha*; other manuscripts *Bethsaida* [e] *3* Some less important manuscripts *paralyzed—and they waited for the moving of the waters. 4From time to time an angel of the Lord would come down and stir up the waters. The first one into the pool after each such disturbance would be cured of whatever disease he had.*

**4:53** *believed.* Cf. the aim of this Gospel (20:31).
**4:54** *the second miraculous sign.* There had, of course, already been many such signs (2:23; 3:2), but this was the second time Jesus performed a sign after coming from Judea to Galilee.
**5:1** *Some time later.* An indefinite expression (cf. 6:1; 7:1). *a feast of the Jews.* Probably one of the three pilgrimage feasts to which all Jewish males were expected to go—Passover, Pentecost or Tabernacles. The identity of this feast is significant for the attempt to ascertain the number of Passovers included in Jesus' ministry, and thus the number of years his ministry lasted. John explicitly mentions at least three different Passovers. the first in 2:13,23 (see note on 2:13), the second in 6:4 and the third several times (e.g., in 11:55; 12:1). If three Passovers are accepted, the length of Jesus' ministry was between two and three years. However, if the feast of 5:1 was a fourth Passover or assumes that a fourth Passover had come and gone, Jesus' ministry would have lasted between three and four years.
**5:2** *there is.* Not "was." This may mean that the pool was still in existence at the time this was being written, i.e., that John wrote before the destruction of Jerusalem. However, this falls short of proving the time of writing (see Introduction: Date). *Bethesda.* The manuscripts have a variety of names (see NIV text note), but one of the Dead Sea Scrolls seems to show that Bethesda is the right name. The site is generally identified with the twin pools near the present-day Saint Anne's Church. There would have been a colonnade on each of the four sides and another between the two pools.
**5:3–4** See NIV text note. Verse 4 was doubtless inserted by a later copyist to explain why people waited by the pool in large numbers.
**5:5** *invalid.* John does not say what the trouble was, but it was a form of paralysis or at least lameness.
**5:6** *Do you want to get well?* The question was important. The man had not asked Jesus for help, and a beggar of that day could lose a sometimes profitable (and easy) income if he were cured. Or perhaps he had simply lost the will to be cured.
**5:7** *when the water is stirred.* The man did not see Jesus as a potential healer, and his mind was set on the supposed curative powers of the water.
**5:9** *the man was cured.* Ordinarily, faith in Jesus was essential to the cure (e.g., Mk 5:34), but here the man did not even know who Jesus was (v. 13). Jesus usually healed in response to faith, but he was not limited by a person's lack of it.
**5:10** *the law forbids you to carry your mat.* It was not the law of Moses but their traditional interpretation of it that prohibited carrying loads of any kind on the Sabbath. The Jews had very strict regulations on keeping the Sabbath, but also had many curious loopholes that their lawyers made full use of (cf. Mt 23:4).
**5:12** *this fellow.* The Jews were contrasting the authority of the law of God, which in their view prohibited the action, and that of a mere man (as they considered Jesus to be) who permitted it.
**5:14** *something worse.* The eternal consequences of sin are more serious than any physical ailment.
**5:16** *was doing.* The continuous action points to more than one incident, and the Jews apparently discerned a pattern. *persecuted.* John does not tell us what form the persecution took.
**5:17** *My Father is always at his work.* Jesus' justification for

always at his work[g] to this very day, and I,
too, am working." 18For this reason the
Jews tried all the harder to kill him;[h] not
only was he breaking the Sabbath, but he
was even calling God his own Father,
making himself equal with God.[i]
19Jesus gave them this answer: "I tell
you the truth, the Son can do nothing by
himself;[j] he can do only what he sees his
Father doing, because whatever the Father
does the Son also does. 20For the Father
loves the Son[k] and shows him all he does.
Yes, to your amazement he will show him
even greater things than these.[l] 21For just
as the Father raises the dead and gives
them life,[m] even so the Son gives life[n] to
whom he is pleased to give it. 22Moreover,
the Father judges no one, but has entrusted all judgment to the Son,[o] 23that all
may honor the Son just as they honor the
Father. He who does not honor the Son
does not honor the Father, who sent him.[p]
24"I tell you the truth, whoever hears
my word and believes him who sent me[q]
has eternal life[r] and will not be condemned;[s] he has crossed over from death
to life.[t] 25I tell you the truth, a time is
coming and has now come[u] when the
dead will hear[v] the voice of the Son of
God and those who hear will live. 26For as
the Father has life in himself, so he has
granted the Son to have life[w] in himself.
27And he has given him authority to
judge[x] because he is the Son of Man.
28"Do not be amazed at this, for a time
is coming[y] when all who are in their
graves will hear his voice 29and come
out—those who have done good will rise
to live, and those who have done evil will
rise to be condemned.[z] 30By myself I can
do nothing;[a] I judge only as I hear, and
my judgment is just,[b] for I seek not to
please myself but him who sent me.[c]

### *Testimonies About Jesus*

31"If I testify about myself, my testimony is not valid.[d] 32There is another who
testifies in my favor,[e] and I know that his
testimony about me is valid.
33"You have sent to John and he has
testified[f] to the truth. 34Not that I accept
human testimony;[g] but I mention it that
you may be saved.[h] 35John was a lamp

**5:17** [g]Jn 9:4; 14:10 **5:18** [h]S Mt 12:14 [i]Jn 10:30,33; 19:7 **5:19** [j]ver 30; S Jn 14:24 **5:20** [k]Jn 3:35 [l]Jn 14:12 **5:21** [m]Ro 4:17; 8:11; 2Co 1:9; Heb 11:19 [n]Jn 11:25 **5:22** [o]ver 27; Ge 18:25; Jdg 11:27; Jn 9:39; S Ac 10:42 **5:23** [p]Lk 10:16; S 1Jn 2:23 **5:24** [q]S Mt 10:40; S Jn 3:15; S 3:17 [r]S Mt 25:46 [s]Jn 3:18 [t]1Jn 3:14 **5:25** [u]Jn 4:23; 16:32 [v]Jn 8:43,47 **5:26** [w]Dt 30:20; Job 10:12; 33:4; Ps 36:9; S Jn 1:4 **5:27** [x]S ver 22 **5:28** [y]Jn 4:21; 16:2 **5:29** [z]S Mt 25:46 **5:30** [a]ver 19 [b]Isa 28:6; Jn 8:16 [c]S Mt 26:39 **5:31** [d]Jn 8:14 **5:32** [e]ver 37; Jn 8:18

**5:33** [f]S Jn 1:7 **5:34** [g]1Jn 5:9 [h]Ac 16:30,31; Eph 2:8; Tit 3:5

his action was his close relation to his Father. The Jews did not refer to God as "My Father," regarding the term as too intimate—though they might have used "Our Father" or, in prayer, "My Father in heaven." Jesus also exemplified the way the Sabbath should be observed. God does not stop his deeds of compassion on that day and neither did Jesus.

**5:18** *his own Father.* Referring to a special relationship. The Jews did not object to the idea that God is the Father of all, but they strongly objected to Jesus' claim that he stood in a special relationship to the Father—a relationship so close as to make himself equal with God.

**5:19** *can.* Because of who and what he was, it was not possible for Jesus to act except in dependence on the Father.

**5:20** *the Father loves the Son.* Therefore the Father revealed to the Son his plans and purposes, and the Son obediently carried them out. *greater things.* The Son's activities in raising the dead and judging (see following verses).

**5:21** *the Father raises the dead.* A firm belief among the Jews. They also held that he did not give this privilege to anyone else. Jesus claimed a prerogative that, according to his opponents, belonged only to God. *the Son gives life.* Probably refers to Christ's gift of abundant life here and now, though possibly also to the future resurrection (see 11:25–26).

**5:22** *entrusted all judgment to the Son.* The Jews believed that the Father is Judge of the world, so this teaching seemed heretical to them.

**5:24** *believes him . . . has eternal life.* Faith and life are connected (cf. 20:31). *has eternal life.* A present possession (see note on 3:15). *has crossed.* The decisive action has taken place, and the believer no longer belongs to death.

**5:25** *is coming and has now come.* A reference not only to the future resurrection but also to the fact that Christ gives life now. The spiritually dead who hear him receive life from him.

**5:26** *has life in himself.* Must be understood against the background of the OT, where life is spoken of as belonging to God and as being his gift (Dt 30:20; Job 10:12; 33:4; Ps 16:11; 27:1; 36:9; etc.). The Son has been given the same kind of life that the Father possesses (cf. also 1Jn 5:11 for the benefit to man).

**5:27** *authority to judge.* Granted to the Son by the Father. *Son of Man.* See note on 1:51.

**5:28–29** A reference to the future raising of the dead.

**5:29** *done good . . . live . . . done evil . . . condemned.* As always in Scripture, judgment is on the basis of works, though salvation, of course, is a gift from God in response to faith (cf. v. 24).

**5:30** *By myself I can do nothing.* Jesus stresses his dependence on the Father (see note on v. 19). He judges only as he hears from the Father, which makes his judgment fair.

**5:31–47** This section stresses the testimonies (see note on 1:7) of John the Baptist (v. 33), of the works of Jesus (v. 36), of God the Father (v. 37), of the Scriptures (v. 39) and of Moses (v. 46).

**5:31** Jesus' testimony about himself required the support of all God's revelation. Otherwise, it would have been unacceptable.

**5:32** *another.* The Father testifies concerning the Son. The Jews might not accept this testimony, but it was the testimony that mattered.

**5:33** *You have sent to John.* A reference to the delegation from the Jewish leaders to John the Baptist (see 1:19). *he has testified.* The testimony of John was important, though not, of course, equal to the testimony of the Father. But had the Jews believed John, they would have believed Christ and would have been saved.

**5:35** *John was.* The past tense may indicate that John was dead or at least imprisoned. In any case, his work was done. *burned and gave light.* John's giving light was costly to him. *for a time.* The Jewish leaders never came to grips with John's message, and their responses to him were always at best tentative and superficial.

that burned and gave light,[i] and you chose for a time to enjoy his light.

36"I have testimony weightier than that of John.[j] For the very work that the Father has given me to finish, and which I am doing,[k] testifies that the Father has sent me.[l] 37And the Father who sent me has himself testified concerning me.[m] You have never heard his voice nor seen his form,[n] 38nor does his word dwell in you,[o] for you do not believe[p] the one he sent.[q] 39You diligently study[f] the Scriptures[r] because you think that by them you possess eternal life.[s] These are the Scriptures that testify about me,[t] 40yet you refuse to come to me[u] to have life.

41"I do not accept praise from men,[v] 42but I know you. I know that you do not have the love of God in your hearts. 43I have come in my Father's name, and you do not accept me; but if someone else comes in his own name, you will accept him. 44How can you believe if you accept praise from one another, yet make no effort to obtain the praise that comes from the only God[g]?[w]

45"But do not think I will accuse you before the Father. Your accuser is Moses,[x] on whom your hopes are set.[y] 46If you believed Moses, you would believe me, for he wrote about me.[z] 47But since you do not believe what he wrote, how are you going to believe what I say?"[a]

## *Jesus Feeds the Five Thousand*

*6:1–13pp — Mt 14:13–21; Mk 6:32–44; Lk 9:10–17*

**6** Some time after this, Jesus crossed to the far shore of the Sea of Galilee (that is, the Sea of Tiberias), 2and a great crowd of people followed him because they saw the miraculous signs[b] he had performed on the sick. 3Then Jesus went up on a mountainside[c] and sat down with his disciples. 4The Jewish Passover Feast[d] was near.

5When Jesus looked up and saw a great crowd coming toward him, he said to Philip,[e] "Where shall we buy bread for these people to eat?" 6He asked this only to test him, for he already had in mind what he was going to do.

7Philip answered him, "Eight months' wages[h] would not buy enough bread for each one to have a bite!"

8Another of his disciples, Andrew, Simon Peter's brother,[f] spoke up, 9"Here is a boy with five small barley loaves and two small fish, but how far will they go among so many?"[g]

10Jesus said, "Have the people sit down." There was plenty of grass in that place, and the men sat down, about five thousand of them. 11Jesus then took the loaves, gave thanks,[h] and distributed to those who were seated as much as they wanted. He did the same with the fish.

12When they had all had enough to eat, he said to his disciples, "Gather the pieces that are left over. Let nothing be wasted." 13So they gathered them and filled twelve baskets with the pieces of the five barley loaves left over by those who had eaten.

14After the people saw the miraculous

**5:35** [i]Da 12:3; 2Pe 1:19
**5:36** [j]1Jn 5:9 [k]Jn 14:11; 15:24 [l]S Jn 3:17
**5:37** [m]Jn 8:18 [n]Dt 4:12; 1Ti 1:17; S Jn 1:18
**5:38** [o]1Jn 1:10; 2:14 [p]Isa 26:10 [q]S Jn 3:17
**5:39** [r]Ro 2:17,18 [s]S Mt 25:46 [t]S Lk 24:27,44; Ac 13:27
**5:40** [u]Jn 6:44
**5:41** [v]ver 44
**5:44** [w]S Ro 2:29
**5:45** [x]Jn 9:28 [y]Ro 2:17
**5:46** [z]Ge 3:15; S Lk 24:27,44; Ac 26:22
**5:47** [a]Lk 16:29, 31
**6:2** [b]S Jn 2:11
**6:3** [c]ver 15
**6:4** [d]S Jn 11:55
**6:5** [e]S Jn 1:43
**6:8** [f]Jn 1:40
**6:9** [g]2Ki 4:43
**6:11** [h]ver 23; S Mt 14:19

[f]*39* Or *Study diligently* (the imperative) [g]*44* Some early manuscripts *the Only One* [h]*7* Greek *two hundred denarii*

**5:36** *work.* The miracles of Jesus, which testified to what he is and to his divine mission (see 10:25).
**5:37** *the Father . . . has himself testified . . . his voice.* Probably a reference to God's voice in the Scriptures (see vv. 38–39). God had also given his voice of approval at Jesus' baptism (see Mt 3:17). *nor seen his form.* Probably refers to their lack of spiritual perception of who Jesus really is.
**5:38** *you do not believe.* The Jews did not recognize what God was saying, as their failure to believe Jesus shows.
**5:39** *You diligently study.* The Jewish leaders studied Scripture in minute detail. Despite their reverence for the very letter of Scripture (see notes on Mt 5:18–21), they did not recognize the one to whom Scripture bears supreme testimony.
**5:41** *praise from men.* Jesus did not accept human praise any more than human testimony (v. 34).
**5:42** *love of God.* May mean God's love for them or theirs for God. Probably it is the latter, but people's love for God is in response to his prior love for them (1Jn 4:19).
**5:43–44** The Jews had their attention firmly fixed on people. Their emphasis on self-seeking and on human praise showed that they did not accept the one who came from God, and therefore they missed the praise that comes from God.
**5:45** *Your accuser is Moses.* The Jews prided themselves on their attachment to Moses, their great lawgiver. So it was an unexpected thrust for Jesus to say that Moses himself would accuse them before God.
**5:46** *he wrote about me.* All the NT writers stressed, or assumed, that the OT, rightly read, points to Christ (cf. Lk 24:25–27,44). Jesus applied this truth specifically to the writings of Moses (see, e.g., notes on Ge 49:10; Ex 12:21; Lev 16:5; Nu 24:17; Dt 18:15).
**6:1–15** The feeding of the 5,000 is the one miracle, apart from the resurrection, found in all four Gospels. It shows Jesus as the supplier of human need, and sets the stage for his testimony that he is the bread of life (v. 35).
**6:1** *Some time after this.* See 5:1 and note. *Sea of Tiberias.* Probably the official Roman name, while Sea of Galilee was the popular name. The name came from the town of Tiberias (named after the emperor), founded c. A.D. 20, and probably was not much in use during Jesus' ministry.
**6:2** *miraculous signs.* See note on 2:11.
**6:4** *Passover.* See note on 2:13.
**6:5** *Philip.* Since he came from nearby Bethsaida (1:44), it was appropriate to ask him.
**6:9** *barley loaves.* Cheap bread, the food of the poor.
**6:10** *about five thousand.* The number of men; women and children were not included (Mt 14:21).
**6:12** *Gather the pieces.* See note on Mk 6:43.

sign[i] that Jesus did, they began to say,
"Surely this is the Prophet who is to come
into the world."[j] 15Jesus, knowing that
they intended to come and make him
king[k] by force, withdrew again to a mountain by himself.[l]

## *Jesus Walks on the Water*

*6:16–21pp — Mt 14:22–33; Mk 6:47–51*

16When evening came, his disciples
went down to the lake, 17where they got
into a boat and set off across the lake for
Capernaum. By now it was dark, and Jesus
had not yet joined them. 18A strong wind
was blowing and the waters grew rough.
19When they had rowed three or three and
a half miles,[i] they saw Jesus approaching
the boat, walking on the water;[m] and they
were terrified. 20But he said to them, "It is
I; don't be afraid."[n] 21Then they were

6:14 [i]S Jn 2:11 [j]Dt 18:15,18; Mt 11:3; S 21:11
6:15 [k]Jn 18:36 [l]Mt 14:23; Mk 6:46
6:19 [m]Job 9:8
6:20 [n]S Mt 14:27

willing to take him into the boat, and
immediately the boat reached the shore
where they were heading.

22The next day the crowd that had
stayed on the opposite shore of the lake[o]
realized that only one boat had been there,
and that Jesus had not entered it with his
disciples, but that they had gone away
alone.[p] 23Then some boats from Tiberias[q]
landed near the place where the people
had eaten the bread after the Lord had giv-
en thanks.[r] 24Once the crowd realized
that neither Jesus nor his disciples were
there, they got into the boats and went to
Capernaum in search of Jesus.

## *Jesus the Bread of Life*

25When they found him on the other

6:22 [o]ver 2 [p]ver 15-21
6:23 [q]ver 1 [r]ver 11

[i]19 Greek *rowed twenty-five or thirty stadia* (about 5 or 6 kilometers)

---

**6:13** *twelve baskets ... left over.* There was abundant supply.
**6:14** *sign.* It pointed people to the Son of Man and the food for eternal life that he gives (v. 27), but they thought only of the Prophet, i.e., the prophet of Dt 18:15 who would be like Moses (see 1:21 and note). Through Moses, God had provided food and water for the people in the desert, and they expected the Prophet to do no more than this.
**6:15** *make him king by force.* Jesus rejected the world's version of kingship as a temptation of the devil (Mt 4:8–10; see note on Jn 18:36).
**6:19** *three or three and a half miles.* Mark says they were

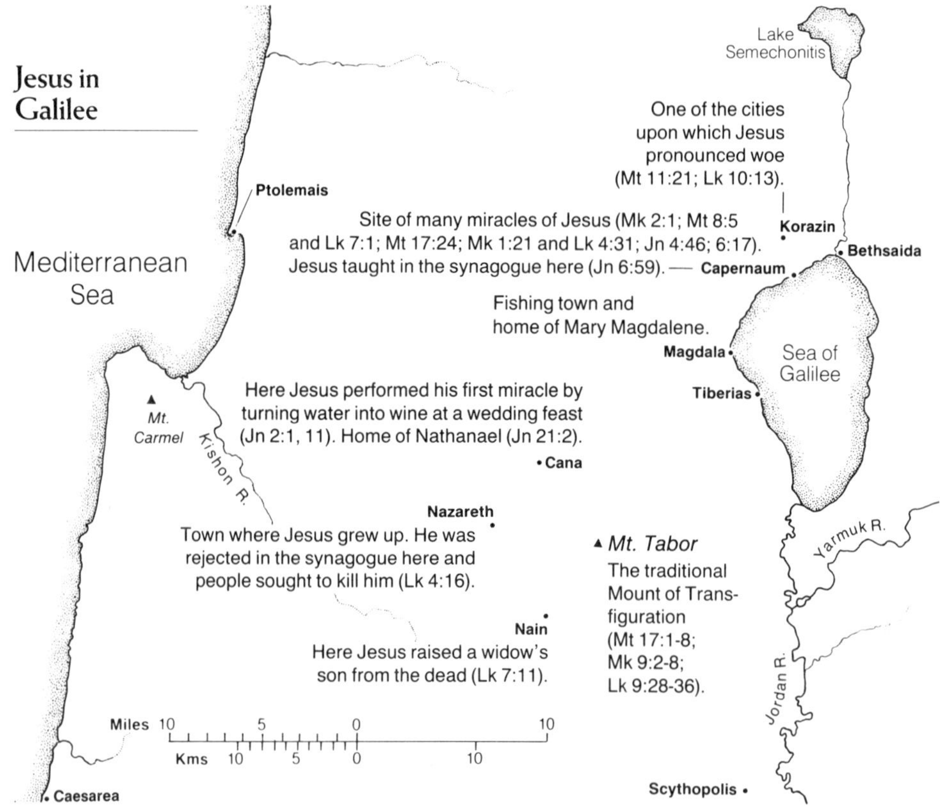

side of the lake, they asked him, "Rabbi,[s]
when did you get here?"

26Jesus answered, "I tell you the truth,
you are looking for me,[t] not because you
saw miraculous signs[u] but because you ate
the loaves and had your fill. 27Do not work
for food that spoils, but for food that en-
dures[v] to eternal life,[w] which the Son of
Man[x] will give you. On him God the Father has placed his seal[y] of approval."

28Then they asked him, "What must we
do to do the works God requires?"

29Jesus answered, "The work of God is
this: to believe[z] in the one he has sent."[a]

30So they asked him, "What miraculous
sign[b] then will you give that we may see it
and believe you?[c] What will you do?
31Our forefathers ate the manna[d] in the
desert; as it is written: 'He gave them
bread from heaven to eat.'[j]"[e]

32Jesus said to them, "I tell you the
truth, it is not Moses who has given you
the bread from heaven, but it is my Father
who gives you the true bread from heaven.
33For the bread of God is he who comes
down from heaven[f] and gives life to the
world."

34"Sir," they said, "from now on give us
this bread."[g]

35Then Jesus declared, "I am[h] the bread
of life.[i] He who comes to me will never
go hungry, and he who believes[j] in me
will never be thirsty.[k] 36But as I told you,
you have seen me and still you do not believe. 37All that the Father gives me[l] will
come to me, and whoever comes to me I
will never drive away. 38For I have come
down from heaven[m] not to do my will but
to do the will[n] of him who sent me.[o]
39And this is the will of him who sent me,
that I shall lose none of all that he has
given me,[p] but raise them up at the last
day.[q] 40For my Father's will is that everyone who looks to the Son[r] and believes in
him shall have eternal life,[s] and I will raise
him up at the last day."

41At this the Jews began to grumble
about him because he said, "I am the
bread that came down from heaven."
42They said, "Is this not Jesus, the son of
Joseph,[t] whose father and mother we
know?[u] How can he now say, 'I came
down from heaven'?"[v]

43"Stop grumbling among yourselves,"
Jesus answered. 44"No one can come to
me unless the Father who sent me draws
him,[w] and I will raise him up at the last
day. 45It is written in the Prophets: 'They

**6:25** [s]S Mt 23:7
**6:26** [t]ver 24 [u]ver 30; S Jn 2:11
**6:27** [v]Isa 55:2 [w]ver 54; S Mt 25:46 [x]S Mt 8:20 [y]Ro 4:11; 1Co 9:2; 2Co 1:22; Eph 1:13; 4:30; 2Ti 2:19; Rev 7:3
**6:29** [z]1Jn 3:23 [a]S Jn 3:17
**6:30** [b]S Jn 2:11 [c]S Mt 12:38
**6:31** [d]Nu 11:7-9 [e]Ex 16:4,15; Ne 9:15; Ps 78:24; 105:40
**6:33** [f]ver 50; Jn 3:13,31
**6:34** [g]Jn 4:15
**6:35** [h]Ex 3:14; Jn 8:12; 10:7,11; 11:25; 14:6; 15:1 [i]ver 48,51 [j]S Jn 3:15 [k]Jn 4:14
**6:37** [l]ver 39; Jn 17:2,6,9,24
**6:38** [m]Jn 3:13,31 [n]S Mt 26:39 [o]S Jn 3:17
**6:39** [p]Isa 27:3; Jer 23:4; Jn 10:28; 17:12; 18:9 [q]ver 40,44, 54
**6:40** [r]Jn 12:45 [s]S Mt 25:46
**6:42** [t]Lk 4:22 [u]Jn 7:27,28 [v]ver 38,62
**6:44** [w]ver 65; Jer 31:3; Jn 12:32

j31 Exodus 16:4; Neh. 9:15; Psalm 78:24,25

"in the middle of the lake" (Mk 6:47). *terrified.* They thought they were seeing a ghost (Mt 14:26).

**6:21** *immediately the boat reached the shore.* Some think that this was another miracle. In any event, the boat's safe arrival is implicitly credited to Jesus.

**6:22–24** The crowd could not figure out what had happened to Jesus. But they wanted to see him again, so they looked for him in the most likely place, Capernaum.

**6:27** *eternal life.* Not something to be achieved but to be received by faith in Christ (see vv. 28–29; see also note on 3:15). *Son of Man.* See note on Mk 8:31. Submission of the Son to the Father is one of John's major themes (see note on 4:34).

**6:28** *What must we do . . . ?* They missed the point that eternal life is Christ's gift and were thinking in terms of achieving it by pious works.

**6:29** *work of God.* Believing in Jesus Christ is the indispensable "work" God calls for—the one that leads to eternal life.

**6:30** *What will you do?* They seek from Jesus a sign greater than the gift of manna that had accompanied Moses' ministry.

**6:31** *manna.* A popular Jewish expectation was that when the Messiah came he would renew the sending of manna. The crowd probably reasoned that Jesus had done little compared to Moses. He had fed 5,000; Moses had fed a nation. He did it once; Moses did it for 40 years. He gave ordinary bread; Moses gave "bread from heaven."

**6:32** Jesus corrected them, pointing out that the manna in the desert did not come from Moses but from God, and that the Father still "gives" (the present tense is important) the true bread from heaven (life through the Son).

**6:33** *the bread of God.* Jesus moved the discussion to something (and Someone) much more important than manna.

**6:34** *this bread.* Probably another misunderstanding, like that by the woman at the well (4:15; cf. also Nicodemus, 3:4). Their minds ran along materialistic lines.

**6:35** *I am.* The first of seven self-descriptions of Jesus introduced by "I am" (see 8:12; 9:5; 10:7,9; 10:11,14; 11:25; 14:6; 15:1,5). In the Greek the words are solemnly emphatic and echo Ex 3:14. *the bread of life.* May mean "the bread that is living" and/or "the bread that gives life." What is implied in v. 33 is now made explicit and repeated with minor variations in vv. 41,48,51.

**6:36** Contrast 20:29.

**6:37** God's action (see v. 44; 10:29; 17:6; 18:9), not man's (v. 28), is primary in salvation, and Christ's mercy is unfailing (see vv. 31–40; 10:28; 17:9,12,15,19; 18:9).

**6:38** *I have come down from heaven.* Repeated six times in this context (vv. 33,38,41,50–51,58), emphasizing Jesus' divine origin. *to do the will of him who sent me.* See note on 4:34.

**6:39** *I shall lose none.* The true believer will persevere because of Christ's firm hold on him (see Php 1:6). *the last day.* An expression found only in John in the NT (see vv. 40,44,54).

**6:40** *eternal life.* See note on 3:15. *raise him up at the last day.* Death cannot destroy the life that Christ gives.

**6:41** *the Jews.* See note on 1:19.

**6:44** *draws.* People do not come to Christ strictly on their own initiative; the Father draws them.

**6:45** *the Prophets.* The section of the OT from which the quotation is taken. *Everyone who . . . learns from him comes.* Only those who learn from God come to salvation, and all who learn from him are saved.

will all be taught by God.'[k][x] Everyone
who listens to the Father and learns from
him comes to me. 46No one has seen the
Father except the one who is from God;[y]
only he has seen the Father. 47I tell you the
truth, he who believes has everlasting
life.[z] 48I am the bread of life.[a] 49Your forefathers ate the manna in the desert, yet
they died.[b] 50But here is the bread that
comes down from heaven,[c] which a man
may eat and not die. 51I am the living
bread[d] that came down from heaven.[e] If
anyone eats of this bread, he will live forever. This bread is my flesh, which I will
give for the life of the world."[f]
52Then the Jews[g] began to argue sharp-
ly among themselves,[h] "How can this
man give us his flesh to eat?"
53Jesus said to them, "I tell you the
truth, unless you eat the flesh[i] of the Son
of Man[j] and drink his blood,[k] you have
no life in you. 54Whoever eats my flesh and
drinks my blood has eternal life, and I will
raise him up at the last day.[l] 55For my
flesh is real food and my blood is real
drink. 56Whoever eats my flesh and drinks
my blood remains in me, and I in him.[m]
57Just as the living Father sent me[n] and I
live because of the Father, so the one who
feeds on me will live because of me. 58This
is the bread that came down from heaven.
Your forefathers ate manna and died, but
he who feeds on this bread will live forever."[o] 59He said this while teaching in
the synagogue in Capernaum.

## *Many Disciples Desert Jesus*

60On hearing it, many of his disciples[p]
said, "This is a hard teaching. Who can
accept it?"[q]
61Aware that his disciples were grumbling about this, Jesus said to them, "Does
this offend you?[r] 62What if you see the
Son of Man[s] ascend to where he was before![t] 63The Spirit gives life;[u] the flesh
counts for nothing. The words I have
spoken to you are spirit[l] and they are life.
64Yet there are some of you who do not
believe." For Jesus had known[v] from the
beginning which of them did not believe
and who would betray him.[w] 65He went
on to say, "This is why I told you that no
one can come to me unless the Father has
enabled him."[x]
66From this time many of his disciples[y]
turned back and no longer followed him.
67"You do not want to leave too, do
you?" Jesus asked the Twelve.[z]
68Simon Peter answered him,[a] "Lord,
to whom shall we go? You have the words
of eternal life.[b] 69We believe and know
that you are the Holy One of God."[c]
70Then Jesus replied, "Have I not chosen you,[d] the Twelve? Yet one of you is a
devil!"[e] 71(He meant Judas, the son of Si-

**6:45** [x]Isa 54:13; Jer 31:33,34; 1Co 2:13; 1Th 4:9; Heb 8:10,11; 10:16; 1Jn 2:27 **6:46** [y]S Jn 1:18; 5:37; 7:29 **6:47** [z]S Mt 25:46 **6:48** [a]ver 35,51 **6:49** [b]ver 31,58 **6:50** [c]ver 33 **6:51** [d]ver 35,48 [e]ver 41,58 [f]Heb 10:10 **6:52** [g]S Jn 1:19 [h]Jn 7:43; 9:16; 10:19 **6:53** [i]Mt 26:26 [j]S Mt 8:20 [k]Mt 26:28 **6:54** [l]ver 39 **6:56** [m]Jn 15:4-7; 1Jn 2:24; 3:24; 4:15 **6:57** [n]S Jn 3:17 **6:58** [o]ver 49-51; Jn 3:36; 5:24 **6:60** [p]ver 66 [q]ver 52 **6:61** [r]Mt 13:57 **6:62** [s]S Mt 8:20 [t]S Mk 16:19; S Jn 3:13; 17:5 **6:63** [u]2Co 3:6 **6:64** [v]S Jn 2:25 [w]S Mt 10:4 **6:65** [x]ver 37,44; S Mt 13:11 **6:66** [y]ver 60 **6:67** [z]Mt 10:2 **6:68** [a]Mt 16:16 [b]ver 63; S Mt 25:46 **6:69** [c]S Mk 1:24; 8:29; Lk 9:20 **6:70** [d]Jn 15:16, 19 [e]Jn 13:27; 17:12

[k]*45* Isaiah 54:13 [l]*63* Or *Spirit*

**6:49** *they died.* Jesus' opponents had set their hearts (cf. v. 31) on that which could neither give nor sustain spiritual life.
**6:50** *eat and not die.* Jesus' gift is in contrast; the life he gives is eternal.
**6:51** *eats of this bread.* Appropriates Jesus as the sustenance of one's life. *my flesh, which I will give.* Looking forward to Calvary. Providing eternal life would be costly to the Giver. *world.* See note on 4:42.
**6:53–58** Jesus' absolute statement that "unless you eat the flesh of the Son of Man and drink his blood, you have no life in you" (v. 53) precludes a direct reference to the Lord's Supper. He clearly does not teach that receiving that sacrament is the one requirement for eternal life or that it is the only ordinance through which Christ and his saving benefits are received. In this very discourse he emphasizes faith in response to testimony (see vv. 35,40,47,51). Flesh and blood here point to Christ as the crucified one and the source of life. Jesus speaks of faith's appropriation of himself as God's appointed sacrifice, not—at least not directly—of any ritual requirement.
**6:54** *the last day.* See note on v. 39.
**6:58** *the bread that came down from heaven.* As in v. 49, the value of the manna is limited and is contrasted with the heavenly food Christ gives. For the tenth time in this chapter reference is made to Jesus' coming down from heaven or to the bread from heaven.
**6:60** *hard.* Hard to accept, not hard to understand. The thought of eating the flesh of the Son of Man and drinking his blood was doubtless shocking to most of Jesus' Jewish hearers (see note on vv. 53–58).
**6:62** *Son of Man.* See notes on Mk 8:31; Lk 6:5; 19:10. *ascend.* Probably refers to the series of events that began with the cross, where Jesus was glorified (see note on 7:39). *where he was before.* Referring to Jesus' heavenly preexistence.
**6:63** Cf. 3:5–6,8. *are spirit and . . . life.* Are the Spirit at work producing life.
**6:65** Coming to Christ for salvation is never a merely human achievement (see vv. 37,39,44–45).
**6:66** *From this time.* May also mean "For this reason" or both. *many . . . turned back.* Jesus had already made clear what discipleship meant, and many were not ready to receive life in the way he taught.
**6:68** As in the Synoptic Gospels, Peter acts as spokesman. *words of eternal life.* The expression is general. Peter was not speaking of a formula but of the thrust of Jesus' teaching. He perceived the truth of v. 63.
**6:69** *We believe and know.* Since the Greek verbs are in the perfect tense, they mean, "We have entered a state of belief and knowledge that has continued until the present time." *the Holy One of God.* Applied to Jesus in Mk 1:24; Lk 4:34 (see Ac 2:27).
**6:70** *a devil.* Judas (v. 71) would oppose Christ in the spirit of Satan.
**6:71** *Iscariot.* Means "a man from Kerioth" (in Judea; see Jos 15:25) and would apply equally to the father and the son (cf. 12:4). Judas seems to have been the only non-Galilean among the Twelve. *one of the Twelve.* And therefore one of the last persons likely to betray Jesus.

mon Iscariot,[f] who, though one of the
Twelve, was later to betray him.)[g]

### Jesus Goes to the Feast of Tabernacles

7 After this, Jesus went around in Galilee, purposely staying away from Judea
because the Jews[h] there were waiting to
take his life.[i] 2But when the Jewish Feast
of Tabernacles[j] was near, 3Jesus' brothers[k] said to him, "You ought to leave here
and go to Judea, so that your disciples may
see the miracles you do. 4No one who
wants to become a public figure acts in
secret. Since you are doing these things,
show yourself to the world." 5For even his
own brothers did not believe in him.[l]

6Therefore Jesus told them, "The right
time[m] for me has not yet come; for you
any time is right. 7The world cannot hate
you, but it hates me[n] because I testify that
what it does is evil.[o] 8You go to the Feast.
I am not yet[m] going up to this Feast, because for me the right time[p] has not yet
come." 9Having said this, he stayed in Galilee.

10However, after his brothers had left for
the Feast, he went also, not publicly, but in
secret. 11Now at the Feast the Jews were
watching for him[q] and asking, "Where is
that man?"

12Among the crowds there was wide-
spread whispering about him. Some said,
"He is a good man."

Others replied, "No, he deceives the
people."[r] 13But no one would say anything publicly about him for fear of the
Jews.[s]

### Jesus Teaches at the Feast

14Not until halfway through the Feast
did Jesus go up to the temple courts and
begin to teach.[t] 15The Jews[u] were
amazed and asked, "How did this man get
such learning[v] without having studied?"[w]

16Jesus answered, "My teaching is not
my own. It comes from him who sent
me.[x] 17If anyone chooses to do God's will,
he will find out[y] whether my teaching
comes from God or whether I speak on my
own. 18He who speaks on his own does so
to gain honor for himself,[z] but he who
works for the honor of the one who sent
him is a man of truth; there is nothing false
about him. 19Has not Moses given you the
law?[a] Yet not one of you keeps the law.
Why are you trying to kill me?"[b]

20"You are demon-possessed,"[c] the

**6:71** [f]S Mt 26:14 [g]S Mt 10:4 **7:1** [h]S Jn 1:19 [i]ver 19,25; S Mt 12:14 **7:2** [j]Lev 23:34; Dt 16:16 **7:3** [k]S Mt 12:46 **7:5** [l]Ps 69:8; Mk 3:21 **7:6** [m]S Mt 26:18 **7:7** [n]Jn 15:18,19 [o]Jn 3:19,20 **7:8** [p]ver 6; S Mt 26:18

**7:11** [q]Jn 11:56 **7:12** [r]ver 40:43 **7:13** [s]Jn 9:22; 12:42; 19:38; 20:19 **7:14** [t]ver 28; S Mt 26:55 **7:15** [u]S Jn 1:19 [v]Ac 26:24 [w]Mt 13:54 **7:16** [x]S Jn 14:24 **7:17** [y]Ps 25:14 **7:18** [z]Jn 5:41; 8:50,54 **7:19** [a]Dt 32:46; Jn 1:17 [b]ver 1; S Mt 12:14 **7:20** [c]S Mk 3:22

[m] *8* Some early manuscripts do not have *yet.*

**7:1–8:59** In chs. 7–8 John records strong opposition to Jesus, including repeated references to threats on his life (7:1,13,19,25,30,32,44; 8:37,40,59). The apostle seems to have gathered the major arguments against the Messiahship of Jesus and here answers them.

**7:1** *After this.* As in 5:1 and 6:1 the time is indefinite. However, 6:4 refers to the Passover Feast and 7:2 to the Feast of Tabernacles, making the interval about six months.

**7:2** *Feast of Tabernacles.* The great feast in the Jewish year, celebrating the completion of harvest and commemorating God's goodness to the people during the desert wanderings (see Lev 23:33–43; Dt 16:13–15; cf. Zec 14:16–19). The name came from the leafy shelters in which people lived throughout the seven days of the Feast.

**7:3** *brothers.* See note on Lk 8:19.

**7:4** It is not clear whether the brothers claimed some knowledge of Jesus' miracles that other people did not have or whether they were suggesting that any claim to Messiahship must be decided in Jerusalem. Their advice was not given sincerely, for they did not believe in Jesus (v. 5).

**7:6** *right time.* Jesus moved in accordance with the will of God (see note on 2:4).

**7:7** *The world.* Either (1) people opposed to God or (2) the human system opposed to God's purposes (see note on 1:10). The brothers belonged to the world and therefore could not be the objects of its hatred. Jesus, however, rebuked the world and was hated accordingly.

**7:8** *not yet.* See NIV text note. Jesus was not refusing to go to the Feast, but refusing to go in the way the brothers suggested—as a pilgrim. When he went, it would be to deliver a prophetic message from God, for which he awaited the "right time" (v. 6).

**7:10** *not publicly.* Rejecting the brothers' suggestion to show himself (v. 4).

**7:12** *whispering.* Because it was not safe to speak openly (cf. v. 13).

**7:14** *halfway through the Feast.* When the crowds would be at their maximum. Teaching in the temple courts at such a time would reach many.

**7:15** *The Jews.* Distinct from "the crowds" (v. 12), who were also Jews (see note on 1:19). *without having studied.* Under a rabbi. Jesus had never been the disciple of a recognized Jewish teacher.

**7:16** *not my own.* The Father, from whom he came, had been his "rabbi" (see note on 4:34).

**7:17** *chooses to do God's will.* Reflecting a whole attitude of life. A person sincerely set on doing God's will welcomes Jesus' teaching and believes in him (cf. 6:29). *he will find out.* Augustine commented, "Understanding is the reward of faith . . . What is 'If any man be willing to do his will'? It is the same thing as to believe."

**7:18** *is a man of truth.* Or "is true." They should recognize that Jesus was not self-seeking. In this Gospel, no one is spoken of as being "true" except God the Father (3:33; 8:26) and Jesus (here). Once more John ranks Jesus with God.

**7:19** *the law.* The Jews congratulated themselves on being the chosen recipients of the law (cf. Ro 2:17), but Jesus told them that they all broke the law of which they were so proud.

**7:20** *You are demon-possessed.* The accusation of demon possession is made elsewhere in John (e.g., 8:48–52; 10:20–21; cf. Mt 12:24–32; Mk 3:22–30). *the crowd.* Probably the pilgrims who had come up to Jerusalem for the Feast—different from "the Jews" who were trying to kill Jesus (v. 1) and the Jerusalem mob that knew of the plot (v. 25).

crowd answered. "Who is trying to kill you?"

21Jesus said to them, "I did one miracle,[d] and you are all astonished. 22Yet, because Moses gave you circumcision[e] (though actually it did not come from Moses, but from the patriarchs),[f] you circumcise a child on the Sabbath. 23Now if a child can be circumcised on the Sabbath so that the law of Moses may not be broken, why are you angry with me for healing the whole man on the Sabbath? 24Stop judging by mere appearances, and make a right judgment."[g]

### *Is Jesus the Christ?*

25At that point some of the people of Jerusalem began to ask, "Isn't this the man they are trying to kill?[h] 26Here he is, speaking publicly, and they are not saying a word to him. Have the authorities[i] really concluded that he is the Christ[n]?[j] 27But we know where this man is from;[k] when the Christ comes, no one will know where he is from."

28Then Jesus, still teaching in the temple courts,[l] cried out, "Yes, you know me, and you know where I am from.[m] I am not here on my own, but he who sent me is true.[n] You do not know him, 29but I know him[o] because I am from him and he sent me."[p]

30At this they tried to seize him, but no one laid a hand on him,[q] because his time had not yet come.[r] 31Still, many in the crowd put their faith in him.[s] They said, "When the Christ comes, will he do more miraculous signs[t] than this man?"

32The Pharisees heard the crowd whispering such things about him. Then the chief priests and the Pharisees sent temple guards to arrest him.

33Jesus said, "I am with you for only a short time,[u] and then I go to the one who sent me.[v] 34You will look for me, but you will not find me; and where I am, you cannot come."[w]

35The Jews said to one another, "Where does this man intend to go that we cannot find him? Will he go where our people live scattered[x] among the Greeks,[y] and teach the Greeks? 36What did he mean when he said, 'You will look for me, but you will not find me,' and 'Where I am, you cannot come'?"[z]

37On the last and greatest day of the Feast,[a] Jesus stood and said in a loud voice, "If anyone is thirsty, let him come to me and drink.[b] 38Whoever believes[c] in me, as[o] the Scripture has said,[d] streams of living water[e] will flow from within him."[f] 39By this he meant the Spirit,[g] whom those who believed in him were later to receive.[h] Up to that time the Spirit

**7:21** [d]ver 23; Jn 5:2-9
**7:22** [e]Lev 12:3 [f]Ge 17:10-14
**7:24** [g]1Sa 16:7; Isa 11:3,4; Jn 8:15; 2Co 10:7
**7:25** [h]ver 1; S Mt 12:14
**7:26** [i]ver 48 [j]Jn 4:29
**7:27** [k]Mt 13:55; Lk 4:22; Jn 6:42
**7:28** [l]ver 14 [m]Jn 8:14 [n]Jn 8:26,42
**7:29** [o]S Mt 11:27 [p]S Jn 3:17
**7:30** [q]ver 32,44; Jn 10:39 [r]S Mt 26:18
**7:31** [s]Jn 8:30; 10:42; 11:45; 12:11,42 [t]S Jn 2:11
**7:33** [u]Jn 12:35; 13:33; 16:16 [v]Jn 16:5,10,17,28
**7:34** [w]ver 36; Jn 8:21; 13:33
**7:35** [x]S Jas 1:1 [y]Jn 12:20; Ac 17:4; 18:4
**7:36** [z]ver 34
**7:37** [a]Lev 23:36 [b]Isa 55:1; Rev 22:17
**7:38** [c]S Jn 3:15 [d]Isa 58:11 [e]S Jn 4:10 [f]S Jn 4:14
**7:39** [g]Joel 2:28; Jn 1:33; Ac 2:17,33 [h]S Jn 20:22

[n]*26* Or *Messiah;* also in verses 27, 31, 41 and 42
[o]*37,38* Or / *If anyone is thirsty, let him come to me. / And let him drink,* 38*who believes in me. / As*

**7:21** *one miracle.* Evidently that of healing the lame man (5:1–9), as the discussion about the Sabbath shows.
**7:22** *circumcision.* The requirement of circumcision was included in the law Moses gave (Ex 12:44,48; Lev 12:3), yet it did not originate with Moses but went back to Abraham (Ge 17:9–14). The Jews took such regulations as that in Lev 12:3 to mean that circumcision must be performed on the eighth day even if it was the Sabbath, a day on which no work should be done. This exception is of critical importance in understanding the controversy (v. 23). Jesus was not saying that the Sabbath should not be observed or that the Jewish regulations were too harsh. He was saying that his opponents did not understand what the Sabbath meant. The command to circumcise showed that sometimes work not only might be done on the Sabbath but must be done then. Deeds of mercy were in this category.
**7:25** *people of Jerusalem.* An expression found only here and in Mk 1:5 in the NT, probably referring to the Jerusalem mob (see note on v. 20). They did not originate the plot against Jesus, but they knew of it.
**7:26** *Have the authorities really concluded . . . ?* In Greek, the question is in a form that expects a negative answer. *the Christ.* See note on 1:25.
**7:27** *no one will know where he is from.* Some Jews held that the OT gave the origin of the Messiah (cf. v. 42; Mt 2:4–6), but others believed that it did not.
**7:28** *you know me.* Irony, because in a sense they knew Jesus and that he came from Nazareth, but in a deeper sense they did not know Jesus or the Father (8:19). Jesus mentioned again his dependence on the Father (cf. 4:34) and went on to declare that he had real knowledge of God and that they did not. Both his origin and mission were from God.
**7:30** *they tried to seize him.* Jesus' enemies were powerless against him until his time came (see note on 2:4).
**7:31** *crowd.* Of pilgrims (see note on v. 20). Many of them believed on the basis of the miraculous signs (cf. 6:26).
**7:32** *the Pharisees.* See notes on Mt 3:7; Mk 2:16; Lk 5:17. *the chief priests.* There was only one ruling chief priest, but the Romans had deposed a number of chief priests, and these retained the title by courtesy.
**7:33** *then I go.* Jesus changed the topic from his miracles to his death, to which he referred enigmatically (v. 34).
**7:35** *scattered among the Greeks.* From the time of the exile, many Jews lived outside Palestine and were found in most cities throughout the Roman empire.
**7:37** *the last . . . day of the Feast.* Either the seventh or the eighth day: This feast lasted seven days (Lev 23:34; Dt 16:13,15) but had a "closing assembly" on the eighth day (Lev 23:36). See note on Mk 14:12. *stood and said in a loud voice.* Teachers usually sat, so Jesus drew special attention to his message.
**7:38** *living water.* See note on 4:10.
**7:39** *the Spirit.* Explaining the "living water" (v. 38). *had not been given.* In the manner in which he would be given at Pentecost (see Ac 2). *glorified.* Here probably refers to Jesus' crucifixion, resurrection and exaltation (see note on 13:31). The fullness of the Spirit's work depends on Jesus' prior work of salvation.

had not been given, since Jesus had not yet
been glorified.[i]
40On hearing his words, some of the
people said, "Surely this man is the
Prophet."[j]
41Others said, "He is the Christ."
Still others asked, "How can the Christ
come from Galilee?[k] 42Does not the Scripture say that the Christ will come from
David's family[p][l] and from Bethlehem,[m]
the town where David lived?" 43Thus the
people were divided[n] because of Jesus.
44Some wanted to seize him, but no one
laid a hand on him.[o]

## *Unbelief of the Jewish Leaders*

45Finally the temple guards went back to
the chief priests and Pharisees, who asked
them, "Why didn't you bring him in?"
46"No one ever spoke the way this man
does,"[p] the guards declared.
47"You mean he has deceived you
also?"[q] the Pharisees retorted. 48"Has any
of the rulers or of the Pharisees believed in
him?[r] 49No! But this mob that knows
nothing of the law—there is a curse on
them."
50Nicodemus,[s] who had gone to Jesus
earlier and who was one of their own
number, asked, 51"Does our law condemn
anyone without first hearing him to find
out what he is doing?"
52They replied, "Are you from Galilee,
too? Look into it, and you will find that a
prophet[q] does not come out of Galilee."[t]

---

[The earliest and most reliable manuscripts and other ancient witnesses do not have John 7:53–8:11.]

53Then each went to his own home.
8 But Jesus went to the Mount of Olives.[u] 2At dawn he appeared again in
the temple courts, where all the people
gathered around him, and he sat down to
teach them.[v] 3The teachers of the law and
the Pharisees brought in a woman caught
in adultery. They made her stand before
the group 4and said to Jesus, "Teacher, this
woman was caught in the act of adultery.
5In the Law Moses commanded us to stone
such women.[w] Now what do you say?"
6They were using this question as a trap,[x]
in order to have a basis for accusing him.[y]
But Jesus bent down and started to
write on the ground with his finger.
7When they kept on questioning him, he

**7:39** [i]Jn 12:23; 13:31,32
**7:40** [j]S Mt 21:11
**7:41** [k]ver 52; Jn 1:46
**7:42** [l]S Mt 1:1 [m]Mic 5:2; Mt 2:5,6; Lk 2:4
**7:43** [n]Jn 6:52; 9:16; 10:19
**7:44** [o]ver 30
**7:46** [p]S Mt 7:28
**7:47** [q]ver 12
**7:48** [r]Jn 12:42
**7:50** [s]Jn 3:1; 19:39
**7:52** [t]ver 41
**8:1** [u]S Mt 21:1
**8:2** [v]ver 20; S Mt 26:55
**8:5** [w]Lev 20:10; Dt 22:22; Job 31:11
**8:6** [x]Mt 22:15,18 [y]S Mt 12:10

[p]42 Greek *seed* [q]52 Two early manuscripts *the Prophet*

---

**7:40** *people.* The "crowd" of v. 20 (see note there).
**7:42** *Bethlehem.* There were different ideas about the Messiah's place of origin (cf. v. 27).
**7:46** *the guards.* They knew they would be in trouble for failing to make the arrest, but did not mention the hostility of part of the crowd, which would have given them something of an excuse before the Pharisees. They were favorably impressed by the teaching of Jesus and were not inclined to cause him trouble.
**7:47** *the Pharisees retorted.* They must have been greatly irritated. Ordinarily the chief priests would have rebuked the temple guards.
**7:49** *this mob.* The pilgrim crowd again (see note on v. 20). *knows nothing.* The Pharisees exaggerated the people's ignorance of Scripture (cf. v. 42). But the average Jew paid little attention to the minutiae that mattered so much to the Pharisees. The "traditions of the elders" were too great a burden for people who earned their living by hard physical work, and consequently these regulations were widely disregarded.
**7:50–51** There is irony here. The Pharisees implied that no leader believed in Jesus, yet Nicodemus, "a member of the Jewish ruling council" (3:1), spoke up. They called for people to observe the law, but Nicodemus pointed to their own failure to keep the law.
**7:52** *a prophet does not come out of Galilee.* See 1:46. They were angry—and wrong. Jonah came from Galilee, and perhaps other prophets as well. Moreover, the Pharisees overlooked the right of God to raise up prophets from wherever he chooses.
**7:53–8:11** This story may not have belonged originally to the Gospel of John. It is absent from almost all the important early manuscripts, and those that have it sometimes place it elsewhere (e.g., after Lk 21:38). But the story may well be authentic.
**7:53** This verse (along with 8:1) shows that the story was originally attached to another narrative, since Jesus was not present at the meeting of the Sanhedrin described in vv. 45–52.
**8:1** *Mount of Olives.* See note on Mk 11:1.
**8:3** *teachers of the law.* See notes on Mt 2:4; Lk 5:17. *a woman caught in adultery.* This sin cannot be committed alone, so the question arises as to why only one offender was brought. The incident was staged to trap Jesus (v. 6), and provision had been made for the man to escape. The woman's accusers must have been especially eager to humiliate her, since they could have kept her in private custody while they spoke to Jesus.
**8:4** *caught in the act.* Compromising circumstances were not sufficient evidence, as Jewish law required witnesses who had seen the act.
**8:5** *to stone such women.* They altered the law a little. The manner of execution was not prescribed unless the woman was a betrothed virgin (Dt 22:23–24). And the law required the execution of both parties (Lev 20:10; Dt 22:22), not just the woman.
**8:6** *using this question as a trap.* The Romans did not allow the Jews to carry out death sentences (18:31), so if Jesus had said to stone her, he could have been in conflict with the Romans. If he had said not to stone her, he could have been accused of being unsupportive of the law. *started to write.* We can only guess what Jesus wrote on the ground.
**8:7** *let him be the first.* Jesus' answer disarmed them. Since he spoke of throwing a stone, he could not be accused of failure to uphold the law. But the qualification for throwing it prevented anyone from acting. *without sin.* The phrase is

straightened up and said to them, "If any
one of you is without sin, let him be the
first to throw a stone[z] at her."[a] 8Again he
stooped down and wrote on the ground.
9At this, those who heard began to go
away one at a time, the older ones first,
until only Jesus was left, with the woman
still standing there. 10Jesus straightened up
and asked her, "Woman, where are they?
Has no one condemned you?"
11"No one, sir," she said.
"Then neither do I condemn you,"[b]
Jesus declared. "Go now and leave your
life of sin."[c]

---

*The Validity of Jesus' Testimony*

12When Jesus spoke again to the people,
he said, "I am[d] the light of the world.[e]
Whoever follows me will never walk in
darkness, but will have the light of life."[f]
13The Pharisees challenged him, "Here
you are, appearing as your own witness;
your testimony is not valid."[g]
14Jesus answered, "Even if I testify on
my own behalf, my testimony is valid, for I
know where I came from and where I am
going.[h] But you have no idea where I
come from[i] or where I am going. 15You
judge by human standards;[j] I pass judgment on no one.[k] 16But if I do judge, my
decisions are right, because I am not alone.
I stand with the Father, who sent me.[l]
17In your own Law it is written that the
testimony of two men is valid.[m] 18I am one
who testifies for myself; my other witness
is the Father, who sent me."[n]
19Then they asked him, "Where is your
father?"
"You do not know me or my Father,"[o]
Jesus replied. "If you knew me, you would
know my Father also."[p] 20He spoke these
words while teaching[q] in the temple area
near the place where the offerings were
put.[r] Yet no one seized him, because his
time had not yet come.[s]
21Once more Jesus said to them, "I am
going away, and you will look for me, and
you will die[t] in your sin. Where I go, you
cannot come."[u]
22This made the Jews ask, "Will he kill
himself? Is that why he says, 'Where I go,
you cannot come'?"
23But he continued, "You are from
below; I am from above. You are of this
world; I am not of this world.[v] 24I told you
that you would die in your sins; if you do
not believe that I am ⌞the one I claim to
be⌟,[r][w] you will indeed die in your sins."
25"Who are you?" they asked.
"Just what I have been claiming all
along," Jesus replied. 26"I have much to
say in judgment of you. But he who sent
me is reliable,[x] and what I have heard
from him I tell the world."[y]
27They did not understand that he was
telling them about his Father. 28So Jesus
said, "When you have lifted up the Son of
Man,[z] then you will know that I am ⌞the
one I claim to be⌟ and that I do nothing on
my own but speak just what the Father has
taught me.[a] 29The one who sent me is
with me; he has not left me alone,[b] for I

**8:7** [z]Dt 17:7; Eze 16:40 [a]Ro 2:1,22 **8:11** [b]Jn 3:17 [c]Jn 5:14 **8:12** [d]S Jn 6:35 [e]S Jn 1:4 [f]Pr 4:18; Mt 5:14 **8:13** [g]Jn 5:31 **8:14** [h]Jn 13:3; 16:28 [i]Jn 7:28; 9:29 **8:15** [j]S Jn 7:24 [k]Jn 3:17 **8:16** [l]Jn 5:30 **8:17** [m]S Mt 18:16 **8:18** [n]Jn 5:37

**8:19** [o]Jn 16:3 [p]S 1Jn 2:23 **8:20** [q]S Mt 26:55 [r]Mk 12:41 [s]S Mt 26:18 **8:21** [t]Eze 3:18 [u]Jn 7:34; 13:33 **8:23** [v]Jn 3:31; 17:14 **8:24** [w]Jn 4:26; 13:19 **8:26** [x]Jn 7:28 [y]Jn 3:32; 15:15 **8:28** [z]S Jn 12:32 [a]S Jn 14:24 **8:29** [b]ver 16; Jn 16:32

[r]*24* Or *I am he*; also in verse 28

---

quite general and means "without any sin," not "without this sin."

**8:9** *began to go away.* Because they were not "without sin" (v. 7). *the older ones.* They were the first to realize what was involved. But all the men were either conscience-stricken or afraid, and in the end only Jesus and the woman remained.

**8:10** *Woman.* Not a harsh form of address (cf. its use in 19:26).

**8:11** *Go now and leave your life of sin.* Jesus did not condone what the woman had done.

**8:12** *I am.* See note on 6:35. *the light.* See 1:4 and note; 9:5; 12:46. It is also true that "God is light" (1Jn 1:5). And as Jesus' followers reflect the light that comes from him, they too are "the light of the world" (Mt 5:14; cf. Php 2:15). *darkness.* Both the darkness of this world and that of Satan. *the light of life.* "God is light" (1Jn 1:5); but Jesus is also the light from God that lights the way for life—as the pillar of fire lighted the way for the Israelites (see Ex 13:21; Ne 9:12).

**8:13** *Pharisees.* See notes on Mt 3:7; Mk 2:16; Lk 5:17.

**8:14** Jesus made two points in reply. First, he was qualified to bear testimony, whereas the Pharisees were not; and he knew both his origin and his destination, whereas they knew neither. (See note on vv. 16–18 for the second point.)

**8:15** The judgment of the Pharisees was limited and worldly. In the sense they meant, Jesus made it clear that he did not judge at all. In the proper sense, of course, he did judge (v. 26).

**8:16–18** Jesus' second point was that his testimony was not unsupported. The Father was with him, so he and the Father were the two witnesses required by the law (Dt 17:6; 19:15).

**8:16** *the Father who sent me.* Jesus was always aware of his mission (see note on 4:34).

**8:19** *If you knew me.* John makes it clear that the Word (Jesus) was with God and was God (1:1) and reveals God (1:18). Jesus here stresses that the Father is known through the Son and that to know the one is to know the other.

**8:20** *his time.* See note on 2:4.

**8:23** Things other than death divide people (cf., e.g., v. 47; 3:31; 15:19; 1Jn 3:10). *of.* Here denotes origin. Jesus was certainly in the world, but he was not of the world. They belonged to "this world"—Satan's domain (1Jn 5:19).

**8:24** *believe.* See note on 1:7. *I am.* Jesus echoes God's great affirmation about himself (see v. 58; see also notes on 6:35; Ex 3:14).

**8:28** *lifted up.* Normally used in the NT in the sense of "exalt," but John uses it of the crucifixion (see 3:14). *Son of Man.* See note on Mk 8:31. *I am.* See notes on vv. 24,58.

always do what pleases him."[c] 30 Even as
he spoke, many put their faith in him.[d]

### The Children of Abraham

31 To the Jews who had believed him,
Jesus said, "If you hold to my teaching,[e]
you are really my disciples. 32 Then you will
know the truth, and the truth will set you
free."[f]

33 They answered him, "We are Abraham's descendants[s][g] and have never
been slaves of anyone. How can you say
that we shall be set free?"

34 Jesus replied, "I tell you the truth,
everyone who sins is a slave to sin.[h]
35 Now a slave has no permanent place in
the family, but a son belongs to it forever.[i]
36 So if the Son sets you free,[j] you will be
free indeed. 37 I know you are Abraham's
descendants. Yet you are ready to kill me,[k]
because you have no room for my word.
38 I am telling you what I have seen in the
Father's presence,[l] and you do what you
have heard from your father.[t]"[m]

39 "Abraham is our father," they answered.

"If you were Abraham's children,"[n]
said Jesus, "then you would[u] do the things
Abraham did. 40 As it is, you are determined to kill me,[o] a man who has told you
the truth that I heard from God.[p] Abraham did not do such things. 41 You are doing the things your own father does."[q]

"We are not illegitimate children," they
protested. "The only Father we have is
God himself."[r]

### The Children of the Devil

42 Jesus said to them, "If God were your
Father, you would love me,[s] for I came
from God[t] and now am here. I have not
come on my own;[u] but he sent me.[v]
43 Why is my language not clear to you?
Because you are unable to hear what I say.
44 You belong to your father, the devil,[w]
and you want to carry out your father's
desire.[x] He was a murderer from the beginning, not holding to the truth, for there
is no truth in him. When he lies, he speaks
his native language, for he is a liar and the
father of lies.[y] 45 Yet because I tell the
truth,[z] you do not believe me! 46 Can any
of you prove me guilty of sin? If I am telling the truth, why don't you believe me?
47 He who belongs to God hears what God
says.[a] The reason you do not hear is that
you do not belong to God."

### The Claims of Jesus About Himself

48 The Jews answered him, "Aren't we
right in saying that you are a Samaritan[b]
and demon-possessed?"[c]

49 "I am not possessed by a demon," said
Jesus, "but I honor my Father and you dis-
honor me. 50 I am not seeking glory for myself;[d] but there is one who seeks it, and he
is the judge. 51 I tell you the truth, if anyone
keeps my word, he will never see death."[e]

52 At this the Jews exclaimed, "Now we
know that you are demon-possessed![f]
Abraham died and so did the prophets, yet
you say that if anyone keeps your word, he
will never taste death. 53 Are you greater
than our father Abraham?[g] He died, and

**8:29** [c]Isa 50:5; Jn 4:34; 5:30; 6:38
**8:30** [d]S Jn 7:31
**8:31** [e]Jn 15:7; 2Jn 9
**8:32** [f]ver 36; Ro 8:2; 2Co 3:17; Gal 5:1,13
**8:33** [g]ver 37,39; S Lk 3:8
**8:34** [h]S Ro 6:16
**8:35** [i]Gal 4:30
**8:36** [j]ver 32
**8:37** [k]ver 39,40
**8:38** [l]Jn 5:19,30; 14:10,24 [m]ver 41,44
**8:39** [n]ver 37; S Lk 3:8
**8:40** [o]S Mt 12:14 [p]ver 26
**8:41** [q]ver 38,44 [r]Isa 63:16; 64:8
**8:42** [s]1Jn 5:1 [t]S Jn 13:3 [u]Jn 7:28 [v]S Jn 3:17
**8:44** [w]1Jn 3:8 [x]ver 38,41 [y]Ge 3:4; 4:9; 2Ch 18:21; Ps 5:6; 12:2
**8:45** [z]Jn 18:37
**8:47** [a]Jn 18:37; 1Jn 4:6
**8:48** [b]S Mt 10:5 [c]ver 52; S Mk 3:22
**8:50** [d]ver 54; Jn 5:41
**8:51** [e]Jn 11:26
**8:52** [f]ver 48; S Mk 3:22
**8:53** [g]ver 39; Jn 4:12

[s]33 Greek *seed;* also in verse 37 [t]38 Or *presence. Therefore do what you have heard from the Father.* [u]39 Some early manuscripts *"If you are Abraham's children," said Jesus, "then*

**8:30** *faith.* Cf. 20:31.
**8:31** *believed.* Here seems to mean "made a formal profession of faith." Their words show that these people were not true believers (see vv. 33,37).
**8:32** *the truth.* Closely connected with Jesus (v. 36; 14:6), it is not philosophical truth but the truth that leads to salvation. *free.* Freedom from sin, not from ignorance (see v. 36).
**8:33** *have never been slaves.* An amazing disregard of their Roman overlords.
**8:34** *a slave to sin.* Because the sinner cannot break free by his own strength.
**8:37** *you are ready to kill me.* See note on 7:1–8:59.
**8:38** Note the contrasts: "I . . . you"; "seen . . . heard"; "the Father . . . your father." Not until later (v. 44) did Jesus say who their father was, but it is clear even at this point that it was neither God nor Abraham as they claimed.
**8:39–41** Their deeds revealed their parentage.
**8:41** *illegitimate.* May have been a slander aimed at Jesus' virgin birth.
**8:43** *my language.* The form of expression—the actual words. *what I say.* The content. The Jews were so convinced of their own preconceptions that they did not really hear what Jesus was saying (cf. v. 47).
**8:44** *your father, the devil.* The Jews' relationship to Satan was now stated explicitly. Jesus clearly excluded the idea of the universal fatherhood of God. *you want.* Points to determination of will. Their problem was basically spiritual, not intellectual. Being oriented toward Satan, they were bent on murder (v. 37) and eventually would succeed (v. 28). *truth.* Foreign to Satan and those who are his (see 14:6).
**8:46** *Can . . . you prove me guilty of sin?* The asking of the question was more significant than the Jews' failure to answer, in that it showed Jesus had a perfectly clear conscience.
**8:47** *hears what God says.* See 10:3–4; 1Jn 4:6.
**8:48** *The Jews.* See note on 1:19. *a Samaritan.* Probably to suggest that he was lax in Jewish observances—"No better than a Samaritan." Or it may be a reflection on the birth of Jesus—perhaps claiming that his father was a Samaritan. *demon-possessed.* See 10:20 and note on 7:20.
**8:51** *my word.* The whole of Jesus' message, which when accepted brings deliverance from death.
**8:53** *Are you greater . . . ?* The question was framed to expect the answer "No." This is ironic, since Jesus was indeed far greater than Abraham, even as he was greater than Moses (see 6:30–35 and notes).

so did the prophets. Who do you think you
are?"
54Jesus replied, "If I glorify myself,[h] my
glory means nothing. My Father, whom
you claim as your God, is the one who
glorifies me.[i] 55Though you do not know
him,[j] I know him.[k] If I said I did not, I
would be a liar like you, but I do know
him and keep his word.[l] 56Your father
Abraham[m] rejoiced at the thought of seeing my day; he saw it[n] and was glad."
57"You are not yet fifty years old," the
Jews said to him, "and you have seen
Abraham!"
58"I tell you the truth," Jesus answered,
"before Abraham was born,[o] I am!"[p] 59At
this, they picked up stones to stone him,[q]
but Jesus hid himself,[r] slipping away from
the temple grounds.

## *Jesus Heals a Man Born Blind*

9 As he went along, he saw a man blind
from birth. 2His disciples asked him,
"Rabbi,[s] who sinned,[t] this man[u] or his
parents,[v] that he was born blind?"
3"Neither this man nor his parents
sinned," said Jesus, "but this happened so
that the work of God might be displayed in
his life.[w] 4As long as it is day,[x] we must do
the work of him who sent me. Night is
coming, when no one can work. 5While I
am in the world, I am the light of the
world."[y]
6Having said this, he spit[z] on the
ground, made some mud with the saliva,
and put it on the man's eyes. 7"Go," he

**8:54** [h]ver 50 [i]Jn 16:14; 17:1,5
**8:55** [j]ver 19 [k]Jn 7:28,29 [l]Jn 15:10
**8:56** [m]ver 37,39; Ge 18:18 [n]S Mt 13:17
**8:58** [o]S Jn 1:2 [p]Ex 3:14; 6:3
**8:59** [q]Ex 17:4; Lev 24:16; 1Sa 30:6; Jn 10:31; 11:8 [r]Jn 12:36
**9:2** [s]S Mt 23:7 [t]ver 34; Lk 13:2; Ac 28:4 [u]Eze 18:20 [v]Ex 20:5; Job 21:19
**9:3** [w]Jn 11:4
**9:4** [x]Jn 11:9; 12:35
**9:5** [y]S Jn 1:4
**9:6** [z]Mk 7:33; 8:23

**9:7** [a]ver 11; 2Ki 5:10; Lk 13:4 [b]Isa 35:5; Jn 11:37
**9:8** [c]Ac 3:2,10
**9:11** [d]ver 7
**9:14** [e]Mt 12:1-14; Jn 5:9
**9:15** [f]ver 10
**9:16** [g]S Mt 12:2 [h]S Jn 2:11 [i]S Jn 6:52

told him, "wash in the Pool of Siloam"[a]
(this word means Sent). So the man went
and washed, and came home seeing.[b]
8His neighbors and those who had for-
merly seen him begging asked, "Isn't this
the same man who used to sit and beg?"[c]
9Some claimed that he was.
Others said, "No, he only looks like
him."
But he himself insisted, "I am the man."
10"How then were your eyes opened?"
they demanded.
11He replied, "The man they call Jesus
made some mud and put it on my eyes. He
told me to go to Siloam and wash. So I
went and washed, and then I could see."[d]
12"Where is this man?" they asked him.
"I don't know," he said.

## *The Pharisees Investigate the Healing*

13They brought to the Pharisees the man
who had been blind. 14Now the day on
which Jesus had made the mud and
opened the man's eyes was a Sabbath.[e]
15Therefore the Pharisees also asked him
how he had received his sight.[f] "He put
mud on my eyes," the man replied, "and I
washed, and now I see."
16Some of the Pharisees said, "This man
is not from God, for he does not keep the
Sabbath."[g]
But others asked, "How can a sinner do
such miraculous signs?"[h] So they were divided.[i]
17Finally they turned again to the blind

**8:56** *my day.* All that was involved in the incarnation. Jesus probably was not referring to any one occasion but to Abraham's general joy in the fulfilling of the purposes of God in Christ, by which all nations on earth would receive blessing (Ge 18:18). *he saw it.* In faith, from afar.
**8:57** *not yet fifty years old.* A generous allowance for Jesus' maximum possible age. Jesus was about 30 when he began his ministry (Lk 3:23).
**8:58** *I am!* A solemnly emphatic declaration echoing God's great affirmation in Ex 3:14 (see vv. 24,28; see also note on 6:35). Jesus did not say "I was" but "I am," expressing the eternity of his being and his oneness with the Father (see 1:1). With this climactic statement Jesus concludes his speech that began with the related claim, "I am the light of the world" (v. 12).
**8:59** *to stone him.* The Jews could not interpret Jesus' claim as other than blasphemy, for which stoning was the proper penalty (Lev 24:16).
**9:1–12** Jesus performed more miracles of this kind than of any other. Giving sight to the blind was predicted as a Messianic activity (Isa 29:18; 35:5; 42:7). Thus these miracles were additional evidence that Jesus was the Messiah (20:31).
**9:2** *who sinned . . . ?* The rabbis had developed the principle that "There is no death without sin, and there is no suffering without iniquity." They were even capable of thinking that a child could sin in the womb or that its soul might have sinned in a preexistent state. They also held that terrible punishments came on certain people because of the sin of their parents. As the next verse shows, Jesus plainly contradicted these beliefs.
**9:4** *we.* Not Jesus only.
**9:5** *the light of the world.* See note on 8:12.
**9:6** Jesus used variety in his cures.
**9:7** *Siloam.* Already an ancient name (see NIV text note on Ne 3:15; see also Isa 8:6). A rock-cut pool on the southern end of the main ridge on which Jerusalem was built, it served as part of the major water system developed by King Hezekiah. *Sent.* Or "one who has been sent."
**9:8** *begging.* Not mentioned previously, but it was about the only way a blind person of that day could support himself.
**9:13** *Pharisees.* See notes on Mt 3:7; Mk 2:16; Lk 5:17.
**9:14** *Sabbath.* Cf. 5:16 and the discussion that follows.
**9:16** *Some . . . others.* The first group started from their entrenched position and ruled out the possibility of Jesus' being from God. The second started from the fact of the "miraculous signs" and ruled out the possibility of his being a sinner (cf. vv. 31–33).
**9:17** *What have you to say about him?* It is curious that they put such a question to such a person; their doing so reflected their perplexity. *a prophet.* Probably the highest designation of which the man could think. He progressed in his thinking about Jesus: from a man (v. 11), to a prophet (v. 17) who might be followed by disciples (v. 27), to one "from

man, "What have you to say about him? It was your eyes he opened."

The man replied, "He is a prophet."[j]

18The Jews[k] still did not believe that he had been blind and had received his sight until they sent for the man's parents. 19"Is this your son?" they asked. "Is this the one you say was born blind? How is it that now he can see?"

20"We know he is our son," the parents answered, "and we know he was born blind. 21But how he can see now, or who opened his eyes, we don't know. Ask him. He is of age; he will speak for himself." 22His parents said this because they were afraid of the Jews,[l] for already the Jews had decided that anyone who acknowledged that Jesus was the Christ[v] would be put out[m] of the synagogue.[n] 23That was why his parents said, "He is of age; ask him."[o]

24A second time they summoned the man who had been blind. "Give glory to God,[w]"[p] they said. "We know this man is a sinner."[q]

25He replied, "Whether he is a sinner or not, I don't know. One thing I do know. I was blind but now I see!"

26Then they asked him, "What did he do to you? How did he open your eyes?"

27He answered, "I have told you already[r] and you did not listen. Why do you want to hear it again? Do you want to become his disciples, too?"

28Then they hurled insults at him and said, "You are this fellow's disciple! We are disciples of Moses![s] 29We know that God spoke to Moses, but as for this fellow, we don't even know where he comes from."[t]

30The man answered, "Now that is remarkable! You don't know where he comes from, yet he opened my eyes. 31We know that God does not listen to sinners. He listens to the godly man who does his will.[u] 32Nobody has ever heard of opening the eyes of a man born blind. 33If this man were not from God,[v] he could do nothing."

34To this they replied, "You were steeped in sin at birth;[w] how dare you lecture us!" And they threw him out.[x]

### *Spiritual Blindness*

35Jesus heard that they had thrown him out, and when he found him, he said, "Do you believe[y] in the Son of Man?"[z]

36"Who is he, sir?" the man asked. "Tell me so that I may believe in him."[a]

37Jesus said, "You have now seen him; in fact, he is the one speaking with you."[b]

38Then the man said, "Lord, I believe," and he worshiped him.[c]

39Jesus said, "For judgment[d] I have come into this world,[e] so that the blind will see[f] and those who see will become blind."[g]

40Some Pharisees who were with him heard him say this and asked, "What? Are we blind too?"[h]

41Jesus said, "If you were blind, you would not be guilty of sin; but now that you claim you can see, your guilt remains.[i]

### *The Shepherd and His Flock*

10 "I tell you the truth, the man who does not enter the sheep pen by

**9:17** [j]S Mt 21:11
**9:18** [k]S Jn 1:19
**9:22** [l]S Jn 7:13 [m]ver 34; Lk 6:22 [n]Jn 12:42; 16:2
**9:23** [o]ver 21
**9:24** [p]Jos 7:19 [q]ver 16
**9:27** [r]ver 15
**9:28** [s]Jn 5:45
**9:29** [t]Jn 8:14
**9:31** [u]Ge 18:23-32; Ps 34:15,16; 66:18; 145:19,20; Pr 15:29; Isa 1:15; 59:1,2; Jn 15:7; Jas 5:16-18; 1Jn 5:14,15
**9:33** [v]ver 16; Jn 3:2
**9:34** [w]ver 2 [x]ver 22,35; Isa 66:5
**9:35** [y]S Jn 3:15 [z]S Mt 8:20
**9:36** [a]Ro 10:14
**9:37** [b]Jn 4:26
**9:38** [c]Mt 28:9
**9:39** [d]S Jn 5:22 [e]Jn 3:19; 12:47 [f]Lk 4:18 [g]Mt 13:13
**9:40** [h]Ro 2:19
**9:41** [i]Jn 15:22,24

[v]*22* Or *Messiah* [w]*24* A solemn charge to tell the truth (see Joshua 7:19)

God" (v. 33), to one who was properly to be worshiped (v. 38).

**9:18** *The Jews.* See note on 1:19. In their prejudice they did not learn from the sign but tried to discredit the miracle.

**9:21** *He is of age.* There was much to which the parents could not testify, but their emphasis on the son's responsibility showed their fear of getting involved.

**9:22** *put out of the synagogue.* Excommunication is reported as early as the time of Ezra (10:8), but there is practically no information about the way it was practiced in NT times. The synagogue was the center of Jewish community life, so excommunication cut a person off from many social relationships (though, in some of its forms, at least in later times, not from worship).

**9:24** *We.* Emphatic in the Greek.

**9:27** *his disciples, too.* The man already counted himself a disciple.

**9:30–33** Good reasoning from an unschooled man.

**9:31** *God does not listen to sinners.* Cf. the remark of some of the Pharisees in v. 16.

**9:34** *threw him out.* May mean "expelled him from their assembly" or, more probably, "excommunicated him" (see note on v. 22).

**9:35** *when he found him.* Jesus obviously had been looking for the man. *Son of Man.* See note on Mk 8:31.

**9:36** The man was ready to follow any suggestion from his benefactor.

**9:38** *I believe.* See 20:31 and note on 1:7. *Lord . . . he worshiped him.* The man was giving Jesus the reverence due to God.

**9:39** It is unlikely that the conversation of vv. 35–38 took place in the presence of the Pharisees. The incident of vv. 39–41, therefore, probably occurred a little later. *For judgment.* In a sense Jesus did not come for judgment (3:17; 12:47), but his coming divides people, and this always brings a type of judgment. Those who reject his gift end up "blind."

**9:40** *Pharisees.* They found it incredible that anyone would consider them spiritually blind.

**9:41** The Pharisees' claim to sight showed their complete unawareness of their spiritual blindness and need. And, though they claimed to have sight, their actions were evidence of their blindness.

**10:1–30** Should be understood in light of the OT (and ancient Near Eastern) concept of "shepherd," symbolizing a

the gate, but climbs in by some other way,
is a thief and a robber.[j] 2The man who
enters by the gate is the shepherd of his
sheep.[k] 3The watchman opens the gate for
him, and the sheep listen to his voice.[l] He
calls his own sheep by name and leads
them out.[m] 4When he has brought out all
his own, he goes on ahead of them, and his
sheep follow him because they know his
voice.[n] 5But they will never follow a
stranger; in fact, they will run away from
him because they do not recognize a
stranger's voice." 6Jesus used this figure of
speech,[o] but they did not understand
what he was telling them.[p]

7Therefore Jesus said again, "I tell you
the truth, I am[q] the gate[r] for the sheep.
8All who ever came before me[s] were
thieves and robbers,[t] but the sheep did
not listen to them. 9I am the gate; whoever
enters through me will be saved.[x] He will
come in and go out, and find pasture.
10The thief comes only to steal and kill and
destroy; I have come that they may have
life,[u] and have it to the full.[v]

11"I am[w] the good shepherd.[x] The good
shepherd lays down his life for the sheep.[y]
12The hired hand is not the shepherd who
owns the sheep. So when he sees the wolf
coming, he abandons the sheep and runs
away.[z] Then the wolf attacks the flock
and scatters it. 13The man runs away because he is a hired hand and cares nothing
for the sheep.

14"I am the good shepherd;[a] I know my
sheep[b] and my sheep know me— 15just as
the Father knows me and I know the Father[c]—and I lay down my life for the
sheep.[d] 16I have other sheep[e] that are not
of this sheep pen. I must bring them also.
They too will listen to my voice, and there
shall be one flock[f] and one shepherd.[g]
17The reason my Father loves me is that I
lay down my life[h]—only to take it up
again. 18No one takes it from me, but I lay
it down of my own accord.[i] I have authority to lay it down and authority to take
it up again. This command I received from
my Father."[j]

19At these words the Jews were again
divided.[k] 20Many of them said, "He is demon-possessed[l] and raving mad.[m] Why
listen to him?"

21But others said, "These are not the
sayings of a man possessed by a demon.[n]
Can a demon open the eyes of the
blind?"[o]

### *The Unbelief of the Jews*

22Then came the Feast of Dedication[y] at
Jerusalem. It was winter, 23and Jesus was

**10:1** [j]ver 8,10 **10:2** [k]ver 11,14; Mk 6:34 **10:3** [l]ver 4,5,14, 16,27 [m]ver 4,5, 14,16,27 **10:4** [n]S ver 3 **10:6** [o]S Jn 16:25, [p]S Mk 9:32 **10:7** [q]S Jn 6:35 [r]ver 9 **10:8** [s]Jer 23:1,2; Eze 34:2 [t]ver 1 **10:10** [u]S Jn 1:4; 3:15,16; 5:40; 20:31 [v]Ps 65:11; Ro 5:17 **10:11** [w]S Jn 6:35 [x]ver 14; Ps 23:1; Isa 40:11; Eze 34:11-16,23; Mt 2:6; Lk 12:32; Heb 13:20; 1Pe 2:25; 5:4; Rev 7:17 [y]ver 15, 17,18; Jn 15:13; 1Jn 3:16 **10:12** [z]Zec 11:16,17

**10:14** [a]S ver 11 [b]ver 27; Ex 33:12 **10:15** [c]Mt 11:27 [d]ver 11,17,18 **10:16** [e]Isa 56:8; Ac 10:34,35 [f]Jn 11:52; 17:20, 21; Eph 2:11-19 [g]Eze 34:23; 37:24 **10:17** [h]ver 11, 15,18 **10:18** [i]Mt 26:53 [j]Jn 15:10; Php 2:8; Heb 5:8 **10:19** [k]S Jn 6:52 **10:20** [l]S Mk 3:22 [m]2Ki 9:11; Jer 29:26; Mk 3:21

**10:21** [n]S Mt 4:24 [o]Ex 4:11; Jn 9:32,33

[x]9 Or *kept safe* [y]22 That is, Hanukkah

---

royal caretaker of God's people. God himself was called the "Shepherd of Israel" (Ps 80:1; cf. Ps 23:1; Isa 40:10–11; Eze 34:11–16), and he had given great responsibility to the leaders ("shepherds") of Israel, which they failed to respect. God denounced these false shepherds (see Isa 56:9–12; Eze 34) and promised to provide the true Shepherd, the Messiah, to care for the sheep (Eze 34:23).

**10:1** *sheep pen.* A court surrounded by walls but open to the sky, and with only one entrance. The walls kept the sheep from wandering and protected them from wild animals.

**10:3** *The watchman.* Apparently in charge of a large fold, where several flocks were kept. *his voice.* The sheep recognized the voice of their own shepherd and responded only to him. *his own sheep.* The shepherd did not call sheep randomly, but only those that belonged to him.

**10:4** *he goes on ahead.* The Palestinian shepherd led his sheep (he did not drive them), and the sheep followed because they knew his voice.

**10:7** *I am.* See note on 6:35.

**10:8** *All . . . before me.* "False shepherds" like the Pharisees and the chief priests, not the true OT prophets (see note on vv. 1–30).

**10:9** *the gate.* The one way into salvation. Inside there is safety, and one is able to go out and find pasture, i.e., the supply of all needs.

**10:10** *thief.* His interest is in himself. Christ's interest is in his sheep, whom he enables to have life to the full (see note on 1:4).

**10:11** *I am.* See note on 6:35. *lays down his life.* A Palestinian shepherd might risk danger for his sheep (see Ge 31:39; 1Sa 17:34–37), but he expected to come through alive. Jesus said that the good shepherd will die for his sheep.

**10:12** *hired hand.* He is interested in wages, not sheep. In time of danger he runs away because of what he is (v. 13) and abandons the flock to predators.

**10:14** *I know . . . my sheep know.* A deep mutual knowledge, like that of the Father and the Son.

**10:15** *I lay down my life.* See v. 11; the fact of central importance.

**10:16** *other sheep.* These already belonged to Christ, though they had not yet been brought to him. *not of this sheep pen.* Those outside Judaism. Here is a glimpse of the future worldwide scope of the church. *one flock.* All God's people have the same Shepherd (see 17:20–23).

**10:17–18** That Christ would die for his people runs through this section of John's Gospel. Both the love and the plan of the Father are involved, as well as the authority he gave to the Son. Christ obediently chose to die; otherwise, no one would have had the power to kill him.

**10:19** *divided.* See 7:43; 9:16.

**10:20** *demon-possessed.* See note on 7:20.

**10:21** Cf. 9:16.

**10:22** *Feast of Dedication.* The commemoration of the dedication (see NIV text note) of the temple by Judas Maccabeus in December, 165 B.C., after it had been profaned by Antiochus Epiphanes. This was the last great deliverance the Jews had experienced. *It was winter.* A description for those unfamiliar with the Jewish calendar.

**10:23** *Solomon's Colonnade.* See Ac 3:11; 5:12. It was a roofed structure—somewhat similar to a Greek stoa—commonly but erroneously thought to date back to Solomon's time.

in the temple area walking in Solomon's
Colonnade.[p] 24The Jews[q] gathered
around him, saying, "How long will you
keep us in suspense? If you are the
Christ,[z] tell us plainly."[r]
25Jesus answered, "I did tell you,[s] but
you do not believe. The miracles I do in
my Father's name speak for me,[t] 26but
you do not believe because you are not my
sheep.[u] 27My sheep listen to my voice; I
know them,[v] and they follow me.[w] 28I
give them eternal life,[x] and they shall never perish;[y] no one can snatch them out of
my hand.[z] 29My Father, who has given
them to me,[a] is greater than all[a];[b] no one
can snatch them out of my Father's hand.
30I and the Father are one."[c]
31Again the Jews picked up stones to
stone him,[d] 32but Jesus said to them, "I
have shown you many great miracles from
the Father. For which of these do you
stone me?"
33"We are not stoning you for any of
these," replied the Jews, "but for blasphemy, because you, a mere man, claim to
be God."[e]
34Jesus answered them, "Is it not written in your Law,[f] 'I have said you are
gods'[b]?[g] 35If he called them 'gods,' to
whom the word of God[h] came—and the
Scripture cannot be broken[i]— 36what
about the one whom the Father set apart[j]
as his very own[k] and sent into the
world?[l] Why then do you accuse me of
blasphemy because I said, 'I am God's
Son'?[m] 37Do not believe me unless I do
what my Father does.[n] 38But if I do it,
even though you do not believe me, believe the miracles, that you may know and
understand that the Father is in me, and I
in the Father."[o] 39Again they tried to seize
him,[p] but he escaped their grasp.[q]
40Then Jesus went back across the Jordan[r] to the place where John had been
baptizing in the early days. Here he stayed
41and many people came to him. They
said, "Though John never performed a miraculous sign,[s] all that John said about this
man was true."[t] 42And in that place many
believed in Jesus.[u]

## *The Death of Lazarus*

11 Now a man named Lazarus was
sick. He was from Bethany,[v] the
village of Mary and her sister Martha.[w]
2This Mary, whose brother Lazarus now
lay sick, was the same one who poured

**10:23** [p]Ac 3:11; 5:12
**10:24** [q]S Jn 1:19 [r]Lk 22:67; Jn 16:25,29
**10:25** [s]Jn 4:26; 8:58 [t]Jn 5:36; 14:11
**10:26** [u]Jn 8:47
**10:27** [v]ver 14 [w]ver 4
**10:28** [x]S Mt 25:46 [y]Isa 66:22 [z]S Jn 6:39
**10:29** [a]Jn 17:2,6,24 [b]Jn 14:28
**10:30** [c]Dt 6:4; Jn 17:21-23
**10:31** [d]S Jn 8:59
**10:33** [e]Lev 24:16; Mt 26:63-66; Jn 5:18
**10:34** [f]Jn 8:17; 12:34; 15:25; Ro 3:19; 1Co 14:21 [g]Ps 82:6
**10:35** [h]S Heb 4:12 [i]S Mt 5:18
**10:36** [j]Jer 1:5 [k]Jn 6:69 [l]S Jn 3:17 [m]Jn 5:17,18
**10:37** [n]ver 25
**10:38** [o]Jn 14:10,11,20; 17:21
**10:39** [p]Jn 7:30 [q]Lk 4:30; Jn 8:59
**10:40** [r]Jn 1:28
**10:41** [s]S Jn 2:11 [t]Jn 1:26,27,30,34
**10:42** [u]S Jn 7:31
**11:1** [v]S Mt 21:17 [w]Lk 10:38

[z]24 Or *Messiah* [a]29 Many early manuscripts *What my Father has given me is greater than all* [b]34 Psalm 82:6

**10:24** *the Christ.* See note on 1:25 and cf. 20:31. This was the critical question, but it was not easy to answer because of the different ideas of Messiahship then in vogue.
**10:25** *I did tell you.* Jesus had not specifically affirmed his Messiahship except to the Samaritan woman (4:26). He may have meant here that the general thrust of his teaching made his claim clear or that such statements as that in 8:58 were sufficient. Or he may have been referring to the evidence of his whole manner of life (including the miracles)—all he had done in the Father's name (for the name see note on 2:23).
**10:26** *not my sheep.* Their failure to believe arose from what they were.
**10:27** *voice.* Cf. vv. 3–5. *I know them.* Cf. v. 14. *they follow.* Cf. vv. 4–5.
**10:28** *eternal life.* Christ's gift (see note on 3:15). *never perish.* The Greek construction here is a strong denial that the sheep will ever perish. The sheep's security is in the power of the shepherd, who will let no one take them from him.
**10:29** *My Father.* See note on 5:17. *can.* The Father's power ("hand") is greater than that of any enemy, making the sheep completely secure.
**10:30** *one.* The Greek is neuter—"one thing," not "one person." The two are one in essence or nature, but they are not identical persons. This great truth is what warrants Jesus' "I am" declarations (see 8:24,28,58 and note on 6:35; see also 17:21–22).
**10:31** *the Jews.* See note on 1:19. *to stone him.* They took Jesus' words as blasphemy, and therefore prepared to carry out the law (Lev 24:16), though without due process.
**10:32** *great miracles.* Or "good deeds" (as, e.g., in Mt 5:16; 1Ti 5:10,25; 6:18). Although the reference here includes Jesus' miracles, the underlying Greek words refer to works in general that are fine and noble in character first of all (see note on v. 38).
**10:33** *blasphemy.* The Jewish leaders correctly understood the thrust of Jesus' words, but their preconceptions and unbelief prevented them from accepting his claim as true.
**10:34** *your Law.* In its strictest sense the term meant the Pentateuch, but was often used, as here, of the whole OT. *you are gods.* The words Jesus quotes from Ps 82:6 refer to the judges (or other leaders or rulers), whose tasks were divinely appointed (see Ex 22:28 and NIV text note; Dt 1:17; 16:18; 2Ch 19:6).
**10:35** *Scripture cannot be broken.* Jesus testified to the complete authority and reliability of the OT.
**10:36** If there is any sense in which men can be spoken of as "gods" (as Ps 82:6 speaks of human rulers or judges), how much more may the term be used of him whom the Father set apart and sent!
**10:37** *what my Father does.* The kind of works of compassion that the Father himself does.
**10:38** *miracles.* Lit. "works." The miracles were a part of Jesus' works. It was Jesus' quality of life, not people's inability to explain his marvels, that he primarily spoke of here (see note on v. 32).
**10:39** *they tried to seize him.* It is not clear if this was to arrest him for trial or to take him out for stoning. *he escaped.* John does not say why they failed, but he often makes it clear that Jesus could not be killed before the appointed time (see note on 2:4; see also Lk 4:30).
**10:41** *all that John said.* For John the Baptist as a witness see 1:7 and note.
**11:1** *Lazarus.* Mentioned only in chs. 11–12 of John's Gospel (the name is found also in the parable of Lk 16:19–31). The sisters are mentioned in Lk 10:38–42
**11:2** *poured perfume.* See 12:3.

perfume on the Lord and wiped his feet
with her hair.[x] 3So the sisters sent word to
Jesus, "Lord, the one you love[y] is sick."
4When he heard this, Jesus said, "This
sickness will not end in death. No, it is for
God's glory[z] so that God's Son may be
glorified through it." 5Jesus loved Martha
and her sister and Lazarus. 6Yet when he
heard that Lazarus was sick, he stayed
where he was two more days.
7Then he said to his disciples, "Let us go
back to Judea."[a]
8"But Rabbi,"[b] they said, "a short while
ago the Jews tried to stone you,[c] and yet
you are going back there?"
9Jesus answered, "Are there not twelve
hours of daylight? A man who walks by
day will not stumble, for he sees by this
world's light.[d] 10It is when he walks by
night that he stumbles, for he has no
light."
11After he had said this, he went on to
tell them, "Our friend[e] Lazarus has fallen
asleep;[f] but I am going there to wake him
up."
12His disciples replied, "Lord, if he
sleeps, he will get better." 13Jesus had
been speaking of his death, but his disciples thought he meant natural sleep.[g]
14So then he told them plainly, "Lazarus
is dead, 15and for your sake I am glad I was
not there, so that you may believe. But let
us go to him."
16Then Thomas[h] (called Didymus) said
to the rest of the disciples, "Let us also go,
that we may die with him."

*Jesus Comforts the Sisters*

17On his arrival, Jesus found that Lazarus had already been in the tomb for four
days.[i] 18Bethany[j] was less than two
miles[c] from Jerusalem, 19and many Jews
had come to Martha and Mary to comfort
them in the loss of their brother.[k] 20When
Martha heard that Jesus was coming, she
went out to meet him, but Mary stayed at
home.[l]
21"Lord," Martha said to Jesus, "if you
had been here, my brother would not have
died.[m] 22But I know that even now God
will give you whatever you ask."[n]
23Jesus said to her, "Your brother will
rise again."
24Martha answered, "I know he will rise
again in the resurrection[o] at the last
day."[p]
25Jesus said to her, "I am[q] the resurrection and the life.[r] He who believes[s] in me
will live, even though he dies; 26and whoever lives and believes[t] in me will never
die.[u] Do you believe this?"
27"Yes, Lord," she told him, "I believe
that you are the Christ,[d][v] the Son of
God,[w] who was to come into the world."[x]
28And after she had said this, she went
back and called her sister Mary aside. "The

**11:2** [x]Mk 14:3; Lk 7:38; Jn 12:3
**11:3** [y]ver 5,36
**11:4** [z]ver 40
**11:7** [a]Jn 10:40
**11:8** [b]S Mt 23:7 [c]Jn 8:59; 10:31
**11:9** [d]Jn 9:4; 12:35
**11:11** [e]ver 3 [f]S Mt 9:24
**11:13** [g]Mt 9:24
**11:16** [h]Mt 10:3; Jn 14:5; 20:24-28; 21:2; Ac 1:13
**11:17** [i]ver 6,39
**11:18** [j]ver 1; S Mt 21:17
**11:19** [k]ver 31; Job 2:11
**11:20** [l]Lk 10:38-42
**11:21** [m]ver 32,37
**11:22** [n]ver 41,42
**11:24** [o]Da 12:2; Jn 5:28,29; Ac 24:15 [p]Jn 6:39,40
**11:25** [q]S Jn 6:35 [r]S Jn 1:4 [s]S Jn 3:15
**11:26** [t]S Jn 3:15 [u]S Mt 25:46
**11:27** [v]S Lk 2:11 [w]S Mt 4:3 [x]Jn 6:14

c *18* Greek *fifteen stadia* (about 3 kilometers) d *27* Or *Messiah*

**11:3** *the one you love.* The relationship must have been exceptionally close.
**11:4** Cf. 9:3. *This sickness will not end in death.* Thus predicting the raising of Lazarus (v. 44), since Jesus already knew of his death (v. 14). In fact, Lazarus must have died shortly after the messengers left Bethany, accounting for the "four days" of vv. 17,39: one day for the journey of the messengers, the two days when Jesus remained where he was (v. 6; see 10:40), and a day for Jesus' journey to Bethany. But see note on v. 17. *glory.* See notes on 7:39; 12:41; 13:31. Here God's Son would be glorified through what happened to Lazarus, partly because the miracle displays the glory of God (who alone can raise the dead; see 5:21) in Jesus (v. 40) and partly because it would help initiate events leading to the cross (vv. 46–53).
**11:6** *he stayed where he was.* Jesus moved as the Father directed, not as people (here Mary and Martha) wished (cf. 2:3–4).
**11:8** *the Jews.* See note on 1:19. *tried to stone you.* See note on 10:31. There was clear danger in going into Judea.
**11:9** *twelve hours.* Enough time for what must be done, but no time for waste.
**11:11** *fallen asleep.* A euphemism for death, used by the unbelieving world as well as by Christians.
**11:15** *believe.* Cf. 20:31.
**11:16** *Thomas . . . Didymus.* The Hebrew word from which we get "Thomas" and the Greek word *Didymus* both mean "twin." We usually remember Thomas for his doubting, but he was also capable of devotion and courage.
**11:17** *four days.* See note on v. 4. Many Jews believed that the soul remained near the body for three days after death in the hope of returning to it. If this idea was in the minds of these people, they obviously thought all hope was gone—Lazarus was irrevocably dead.
**11:18** *less than two miles.* Reflects John's concern for accuracy.
**11:19** *to comfort them.* Jewish custom provided for three days of very heavy mourning, then four of heavy mourning, followed by lighter mourning for the remainder of 30 days. It was usual for friends to visit the family to comfort them.
**11:20** *she went out to meet him.* Perhaps because as the elder she was hostess.
**11:21** Repeated by Mary in v. 32. Perhaps the sisters had said this to one another often as they awaited Jesus' arrival.
**11:22** *whatever you ask.* This comment seems to mean that Martha hoped for an immediate resurrection in spite of the fact that Lazarus's body had already begun to decay. Nothing is too difficult for God to do.
**11:25** *I am.* See note on 6:35. *life.* See note on 1:4. Jesus was saying more than that he gives resurrection and life. In some way these are identified with him, and his nature is such that final death is impossible for him. He is life (cf. 14:6; Ac 3:15; Heb 7:16). *He who believes . . . will live.* See note on 1:7. Jesus not only is life but conveys life to the believer so that death will never triumph over him (cf. 1Co 15:54–57).
**11:27** *I believe.* Martha is often remembered for her shortcoming recorded in Lk 10:40–41. But she was a woman of faith, as this magnificent declaration shows.

Teacher[y] is here," she said, "and is asking
for you." 29When Mary heard this, she got
up quickly and went to him. 30Now Jesus
had not yet entered the village, but was
still at the place where Martha had met
him.[z] 31When the Jews who had been
with Mary in the house, comforting her,[a]
noticed how quickly she got up and went
out, they followed her, supposing she was
going to the tomb to mourn there.
32When Mary reached the place where
Jesus was and saw him, she fell at his feet
and said, "Lord, if you had been here, my
brother would not have died."[b]
33When Jesus saw her weeping, and the
Jews who had come along with her also
weeping, he was deeply moved[c] in spirit
and troubled.[d] 34"Where have you laid
him?" he asked.
"Come and see, Lord," they replied.
35Jesus wept.[e]
36Then the Jews said, "See how he
loved him!"[f]
37But some of them said, "Could not he
who opened the eyes of the blind man[g]
have kept this man from dying?"[h]

### *Jesus Raises Lazarus From the Dead*

38Jesus, once more deeply moved,[i]
came to the tomb. It was a cave with a
stone laid across the entrance.[j] 39"Take
away the stone," he said.
"But, Lord," said Martha, the sister of
the dead man, "by this time there is a bad
odor, for he has been there four days."[k]
40Then Jesus said, "Did I not tell you
that if you believed,[l] you would see the
glory of God?"[m]
41So they took away the stone. Then
Jesus looked up[n] and said, "Father,[o] I
thank you that you have heard me. 42I
knew that you always hear me, but I said
this for the benefit of the people standing
here,[p] that they may believe that you sent
me."[q]
43When he had said this, Jesus called in
a loud voice, "Lazarus, come out!"[r] 44The
dead man came out, his hands and feet
wrapped with strips of linen,[s] and a cloth
around his face.[t]
Jesus said to them, "Take off the grave
clothes and let him go."

### *The Plot to Kill Jesus*

45Therefore many of the Jews who had
come to visit Mary,[u] and had seen what
Jesus did,[v] put their faith in him.[w] 46But
some of them went to the Pharisees and
told them what Jesus had done. 47Then the
chief priests and the Pharisees[x] called a
meeting[y] of the Sanhedrin.[z]
"What are we accomplishing?" they
asked. "Here is this man performing many
miraculous signs.[a] 48If we let him go on
like this, everyone will believe in him, and
then the Romans will come and take away
both our place[e] and our nation."
49Then one of them, named Caiaphas,[b]
who was high priest that year,[c] spoke up,
"You know nothing at all! 50You do not
realize that it is better for you that one

[e]48 Or *temple*

**11:28** [y]Mt 26:18; Jn 13:13 **11:30** [z]ver 20 **11:31** [a]ver 19 **11:32** [b]ver 21 **11:33** [c]ver 38 [d]S Jn 12:27 **11:35** [e]Lk 19:41 **11:36** [f]ver 3 **11:37** [g]Jn 9:6,7 [h]ver 21,32 **11:38** [i]ver 33 [j]Mt 27:60; Lk 24:2; Jn 20:1 **11:39** [k]ver 17 **11:40** [l]ver 23-25 [m]ver 4 **11:41** [n]Jn 17:1 [o]S Mt 11:25 **11:42** [p]Jn 12:30 [q]S Jn 3:17 **11:43** [r]S Lk 7:14 **11:44** [s]Jn 19:40 [t]Jn 20:7 **11:45** [u]ver 19 [v]Jn 2:23 [w]Ex 14:31; S Jn 7:31 **11:47** [x]ver 57 [y]Mt 26:3 [z]S Mt 5:22 [a]S Jn 2:11 **11:49** [b]S Mt 26:3 [c]ver 51; Jn 18:13, 14

**11:28** *The Teacher.* A significant description to be given by a woman. The rabbis would not teach women (cf. 4:27), but Jesus taught them frequently.
**11:31** *to mourn there.* Wailing at a tomb was common, and the Jews immediately thought this was in Mary's mind. Because they followed her, Jesus got maximum publicity.
**11:32** Cf. v. 21.
**11:33** *weeping.* Both times the word denotes a loud expression of grief, i.e., "wailing." *troubled.* See note on 12:27; cf. 13:21.
**11:35** *wept.* The Greek for this word is not the one for loud grief, as in v. 33, but one that denotes quiet weeping, i.e., "shed tears."
**11:36** Cf. v. 5.
**11:37** Their position was like that of Martha (v. 21) and Mary (v. 32), but they based it on Jesus' ability to give sight to the blind (cf. ch. 9).
**11:39** *four days.* See notes on vv. 4,17.
**11:40** *glory.* See note on v. 4.
**11:44** *strips of linen.* Narrow strips, like bandages. Sometimes a shroud was used (see note on 19:40). *a cloth.* A separate item.
**11:45** *many of the Jews . . . put their faith in him.* Perhaps some who had been opposed to Jesus now came to believe (see note on 1:19; cf. 20:31).
**11:46** *Pharisees.* See notes on Mt 3:7; Mk 2:16; Lk 5:17.
**11:47** *the chief priests and the Pharisees.* In all four Gospels the Pharisees appear as Jesus' principal opponents throughout his public ministry. But they lacked political power, and it is the chief priests who were prominent in the events that led to Jesus' crucifixion. Here both groups are associated in a meeting of the Sanhedrin (see note on Mk 14:55). They did not deny the reality of the miraculous signs (see note on 2:11), but they did not understand their meaning, for they failed to believe.
**11:48** *place.* Probably the temple (see NIV text note and Ac 6:13–14; 21:28), though sometimes the Jews used the expression to denote Jerusalem.
**11:49** *Caiaphas.* High priest c. A.D. 18–36. He was the son-in-law of Annas (18:13), who had been deposed from the high priesthood by the Romans in A.D. 15. *high priest that year.* Means "high priest at that time." The high priesthood was not an annual office but one supposed to be held for life. *You know nothing at all!* A remark typical of Sadducean rudeness (Caiaphas, as high priest, was a Sadducee). Josephus says that Sadducees "in their intercourse with their peers are as rude as to aliens." For Sadducees see notes on Mt 2:4; 3:7; Mk 12:18; Lk 20:27; Ac 4:1.
**11:50** *better.* Caiaphas was concerned with political expediency, not with guilt and innocence. He believed that one man, no matter how innocent, should perish rather than that the nation be put in jeopardy. Ironically, the Jews went ahead with their execution of Jesus, and in A.D. 70 the nation still perished.

man die for the people than that the whole
nation perish."[d]
51He did not say this on his own, but as
high priest that year he prophesied that
Jesus would die for the Jewish nation,
52and not only for that nation but also for
the scattered children of God, to bring
them together and make them one.[e] 53So
from that day on they plotted to take his
life.[f]
54Therefore Jesus no longer moved
about publicly among the Jews.[g] Instead
he withdrew to a region near the desert, to
a village called Ephraim, where he stayed
with his disciples.
55When it was almost time for the
Jewish Passover,[h] many went up from the
country to Jerusalem for their ceremonial
cleansing[i] before the Passover. 56They
kept looking for Jesus,[j] and as they stood
in the temple area they asked one another,
"What do you think? Isn't he coming to
the Feast at all?" 57But the chief priests
and Pharisees had given orders that if anyone found out where Jesus was, he should
report it so that they might arrest him.

### *Jesus Anointed at Bethany*

*12:1–8Ref — Mt 26:6–13; Mk 14:3–9; Lk 7:37–39*

12 Six days before the Passover,[k]
Jesus arrived at Bethany,[l] where
Lazarus lived, whom Jesus had raised from
the dead. 2Here a dinner was given in
Jesus' honor. Martha served,[m] while Lazarus was among those reclining at the table
with him. 3Then Mary took about a pint[f]
of pure nard, an expensive perfume;[n] she
poured it on Jesus' feet and wiped his feet
with her hair.[o] And the house was filled
with the fragrance of the perfume.
4But one of his disciples, Judas Iscariot,
who was later to betray him,[p] objected,
5"Why wasn't this perfume sold and the
money given to the poor? It was worth a
year's wages.[g]" 6He did not say this because he cared about the poor but because
he was a thief; as keeper of the money
bag,[q] he used to help himself to what was
put into it.
7"Leave her alone," Jesus replied. "⌊It
was intended⌋ that she should save this
perfume for the day of my burial.[r] 8You
will always have the poor among you,[s]
but you will not always have me."
9Meanwhile a large crowd of Jews found
out that Jesus was there and came, not
only because of him but also to see Lazarus, whom he had raised from the dead.[t]
10So the chief priests made plans to kill
Lazarus as well, 11for on account of him[u]
many of the Jews were going over to Jesus
and putting their faith in him.[v]

### *The Triumphal Entry*

*12:12–15pp — Mt 21:4–9; Mk 11:7–10; Lk 19:35–38*

12The next day the great crowd that had
come for the Feast heard that Jesus was on
his way to Jerusalem. 13They took palm

**11:50** [d]Jn 18:14 **11:52** [e]Isa 49:6; Jn 10:16 **11:53** [f]S Mt 12:14 **11:54** [g]Jn 7:1 **11:55** [h]Ex 12:13, 23,27; Mt 26:1,2; Mk 14:1; Jn 13:1 [i]2Ch 30:17,18 **11:56** [j]Jn 7:11 **12:1** [k]S Jn 11:55 [l]S Mt 21:17 **12:2** [m]Lk 10:38-42 **12:3** [n]Mk 14:3 [o]Jn 11:2 **12:4** [p]S Mt 10:4 **12:6** [q]Jn 13:29 **12:7** [r]Jn 19:40 **12:8** [s]Dt 15:11 **12:9** [t]Jn 11:43,44 **12:11** [u]ver 17, 18; Jn 11:45 [v]S Jn 7:31

[f]3 Greek *a litra* (probably about 0.5 liter) [g]5 Greek *three hundred denarii*

**11:51** *as high priest.* Caiaphas was not a private citizen but was God's high priest, and God overruled in what he said. *prophesied.* His words were true in a way he could not imagine. Prophecy in Scripture is the impartation of divinely revealed truth. In reality Caiaphas's words meant that Jesus' death would be for the nation, not by way of removing political trouble, but by taking away the sins of those who believed in him.
**11:52** *for the scattered children of God.* Jesus' death would have effects far beyond the nation (cf. 1:29; 3:16; 4:42; 10:16; etc.).
**11:54** *he withdrew.* Jesus was not to die before his "time" (see note on 2:4), but he would not act imprudently. Knowing the attitude of his opponents, he withdrew. He would die for others, but in his own time, not that of his enemies. *Ephraim.* If it was the city known as Ophrah, it was about 15 miles north of Jerusalem.
**11:55** *Passover.* See notes on 2:13; 5:1. *ceremonial cleansing.* Especially important at a time like Passover, because without it, it would not be possible to keep the Feast (cf. 18:28; see note on 2:6).
**11:56** *Isn't he coming . . . ?* The question expected the answer "No."
**12:1–11** All four Gospels have an account of a woman anointing Jesus. John's account seems to tell of the same incident recorded in Mt 26:6–13 and Mk 14:3–9, while that in Lk 7:36–50 is different.
**12:1** *Bethany.* See note on Mt 21:17.
**12:3** *nard.* The name of both a plant and the fragrant oil it yielded. Since it was very expensive, Mary's act of devotion was costly. It was also an unusual act, both because she poured the oil on Jesus' feet (normally it was poured on the head) and because she used her hair to wipe them (a respectable woman did not unbind her hair in public). Further, it showed her humility, for it was a servant's work to attend to the feet (see notes on 1:27; 13:5).
**12:4** *Judas Iscariot.* See note on 6:71.
**12:6** *a thief.* The one passage from which we learn that Judas was dishonest. Yet he must have been thought to be a man of some reliability, for he was keeper of the money bag.
**12:7** *save.* Probably the meaning is "save for this purpose." Perfume was normally associated with festivity, but it was also used in burials (see 19:39–40), and Jesus links it with his burial, which Mary's act unwittingly anticipates.
**12:9** *Jews.* See note on 1:19.
**12:10** The Jewish leaders previously had spoken of the death of one man (11:50), but now they wanted another death. Sin grows.
**12:12** *great crowd.* Pilgrims who had come up from the country for the Passover Feast. Many of the pilgrims had doubtless seen and heard Jesus in Galilee, and they welcomed the opportunity to proclaim him as Messiah.
**12:13** *palm branches.* Used in celebration of victory. John saw a multitude with palm branches in heaven (Rev 7:9). *Hosanna!* See NIV text note; see also note on Mt 21:9. *the name.* See note on 2:23. *Blessed is the King of Israel!* The

branches[w] and went out to meet him,
shouting,

"Hosanna![h]"

"Blessed is he who comes in the name
of the Lord!"[i] [x]

"Blessed is the King of Israel!"[y]

14Jesus found a young donkey and sat upon
it, as it is written,

15"Do not be afraid, O Daughter of Zion;
see, your king is coming,
seated on a donkey's colt."[j] [z]

16At first his disciples did not understand
all this.[a] Only after Jesus was glorified[b]
did they realize that these things had been
written about him and that they had done
these things to him.

17Now the crowd that was with him[c]
when he called Lazarus from the tomb and
raised him from the dead continued to
spread the word. 18Many people, because
they had heard that he had given this miraculous sign,[d] went out to meet him. 19So
the Pharisees said to one another, "See,
this is getting us nowhere. Look how the
whole world has gone after him!"[e]

### Jesus Predicts His Death

20Now there were some Greeks[f] among
those who went up to worship at the
Feast. 21They came to Philip, who was
from Bethsaida[g] in Galilee, with a request.
"Sir," they said, "we would like to see
Jesus." 22Philip went to tell Andrew; Andrew and Philip in turn told Jesus.

23Jesus replied, "The hour[h] has come
for the Son of Man to be glorified.[i] 24I tell
you the truth, unless a kernel of wheat falls
to the ground and dies,[j] it remains only a
single seed. But if it dies, it produces many
seeds. 25The man who loves his life will
lose it, while the man who hates his life in
this world will keep it[k] for eternal life.[l]
26Whoever serves me must follow me; and
where I am, my servant also will be.[m] My
Father will honor the one who serves me.

27"Now my heart is troubled,[n] and
what shall I say? 'Father,[o] save me from
this hour'?[p] No, it was for this very reason
I came to this hour. 28Father, glorify your
name!"

Then a voice came from heaven,[q] "I
have glorified it, and will glorify it again."
29The crowd that was there and heard it
said it had thundered; others said an angel
had spoken to him.

30Jesus said, "This voice was for your
benefit,[r] not mine. 31Now is the time for
judgment on this world;[s] now the prince
of this world[t] will be driven out. 32But I,
when I am lifted up from the earth,[u] will
draw all men to myself."[v] 33He said this to
show the kind of death he was going to
die.[w]

34The crowd spoke up, "We have heard

**12:13** [w]Lev 23:40 [x]Ps 118:25,26 [y]S Jn 1:49 **12:15** [z]Zec 9:9 **12:16** [a]S Mk 9:32 [b]ver 23; Jn 2:22; 7:39 **12:17** [c]Jn 11:42 **12:18** [d]ver 11; Lk 19:37 **12:19** [e]Jn 11:47, 48 **12:20** [f]Jn 7:35; Ac 11:20 **12:21** [g]S Mt 11:21 **12:23** [h]S Mt 26:18 [i]Jn 13:32; 17:1 **12:24** [j]1Co 15:36 **12:25** [k]Mt 10:39; Mk 8:35; Lk 14:26; 17:33 [l]S Mt 25:46 **12:26** [m]Jn 14:3; 17:24; 2Co 5:8; Php 1:23; 1Th 4:17 **12:27** [n]Mt 26:38, 39; Jn 11:33,38; 13:21 [o]S Mt 11:25 [p]ver 23 **12:28** [q]S Mt 3:17 **12:30** [r]Ex 19:9; Jn 11:42 **12:31** [s]Jn 16:11 [t]Jn 14:30; 16:11; 2Co 4:4; Eph 2:2; 1Jn 4:4; 5:19 **12:32** [u]ver34; Isa 11:10; Jn 3:14; 8:28 [v]Jn 6:44 **12:33** [w]Jn 18:32; 21:19

[h] *13* A Hebrew expression meaning "Save!" which became an exclamation of praise [i] *13* Psalm 118:25, 26 [j] *15* Zech. 9:9

people's addition to the words of the psalm, which John alone records. It reflects his special interest in Jesus' royalty, which he brings out throughout the passion narrative.
**12:14** *donkey.* See notes on Zec 9:9; Mt 21:2,7; Mk 11:2; Lk 19:30.
**12:16** An example of the meaning of 16:13. *glorified.* See notes on v. 41; 11:4; 13:31. Only after the crucifixion and the coming of the Holy Spirit did the disciples appreciate the meaning of the prophecy and its fulfillment.
**12:19** *Pharisees.* See notes on Mt 3:7; Mk 2:16; Lk 5:17.
**12:20** *Greeks.* Probably "God-fearers," people attracted to Judaism by its monotheism and morality, but repelled by its nationalism and requirements such as circumcision. They worshiped in the synagogues but did not become proselytes.
**12:21** *Philip.* A Greek name, which may be why they came to this disciple (though he was not the only one of the Twelve to have a Greek name). *to see.* Means "to have an interview with." After v. 22 John records no more about these Greeks (yet see note on v. 32). He regarded their coming as important but not their conversation with Jesus. Jesus came to die for the world, and the coming of these Gentiles indicates the scope of the effectiveness of his approaching crucifixion.
**12:23** *The hour has come.* The hour to which everything else led (see note on 2:4). *glorified.* Jesus was speaking about his death on the cross and his subsequent resurrection and exaltation (see notes on v. 41; 11:4; 13:31).
**12:24** *if it dies, it produces.* The principle of life through death is seen in the plant world. The kernel must perish as a kernel if there is to be a plant.
**12:25** *the man who hates his life . . . will keep it.* To love one's life here and now—to concentrate on one's own success—is to lose what matters (cf. Mt 16:24–25; Mk 8:34–35; Lk 9:23–24). Supremely, of course, the principle is seen in the cross of Jesus. *hates.* Love for God must be such that all other loves are, by comparison, hatred. *eternal life.* See note on 3:15.
**12:27** *troubled.* John's equivalent to the agony in Gethsemane described in the other Gospels. *this hour.* Jesus faced the prospect of becoming sin (or a sin offering) for sinful people (2Co 5:21). He considered praying for God to save him from this death, but refused to pray it, because the very reason he had come was to die.
**12:28** *Father, glorify your name!* His prayer was not for deliverance but for the Father to be glorified. The voice from heaven gave the answer. *name.* See note on 2:23.
**12:31** *on this world.* The cross was God's judgment on the world. *the prince of this world.* Satan (cf. 16:11). The cross would seem to be his triumph; in fact, it was his defeat. Out of it would flow the greatest good ever to come to the world.
**12:32** *lifted up.* See note on 3:14. The cross was the supreme exaltation of Jesus (see notes on v. 41; 13:31). *all men.* Christ will draw people to himself without regard for nationality, ethnic affiliation or status. It is significant that Greek Gentiles were present on this occasion (v. 20).
**12:34** *the Law.* Here seems to mean OT Scripture in general (see note on 10:34), the reference being to passages

from the Law[x] that the Christ[k] will remain forever,[y] so how can you say, 'The
Son of Man[z] must be lifted up'?[a] Who is
this 'Son of Man'?"
35 Then Jesus told them, "You are going
to have the light[b] just a little while longer.
Walk while you have the light,[c] before
darkness overtakes you.[d] The man who
walks in the dark does not know where he
is going. 36 Put your trust in the light while
you have it, so that you may become sons
of light."[e] When he had finished speaking,
Jesus left and hid himself from them.[f]

### *The Jews Continue in Their Unbelief*

37 Even after Jesus had done all these miraculous signs[g] in their presence, they still
would not believe in him. 38 This was to
fulfill the word of Isaiah the prophet:

"Lord, who has believed our message
and to whom has the arm of the Lord
been revealed?"[l] [h]

39 For this reason they could not believe,
because, as Isaiah says elsewhere:

40 "He has blinded their eyes
and deadened their hearts,
so they can neither see with their eyes,
nor understand with their hearts,
nor turn—and I would heal
them."[m] [i]

41 Isaiah said this because he saw Jesus'
glory[j] and spoke about him.[k]

42 Yet at the same time many even
among the leaders believed in him.[l] But
because of the Pharisees[m] they would not
confess their faith for fear they would be
put out of the synagogue;[n] 43 for they
loved praise from men[o] more than praise
from God.[p]
44 Then Jesus cried out, "When a man
believes in me, he does not believe in me
only, but in the one who sent me.[q]
45 When he looks at me, he sees the one
who sent me.[r] 46 I have come into the
world as a light,[s] so that no one who believes in me should stay in darkness.
47 "As for the person who hears my
words but does not keep them, I do not
judge him. For I did not come to judge the
world, but to save it.[t] 48 There is a judge
for the one who rejects me and does not
accept my words; that very word which I
spoke will condemn him[u] at the last day.
49 For I did not speak of my own accord,
but the Father who sent me commanded
me[v] what to say and how to say it. 50 I
know that his command leads to eternal
life.[w] So whatever I say is just what the
Father has told me to say."[x]

### *Jesus Washes His Disciples' Feet*

13 It was just before the Passover
Feast.[y] Jesus knew that the time
had come[z] for him to leave this world and
go to the Father.[a] Having loved his own

**12:34** [x]S Jn 10:34 [y]Ps 110:4; Isa 9:7; Eze 37:25; Da 7:14 [z]S Mt 8:20 [a]Jn 3:14 **12:35** [b]ver 46 [c]Eph 5:8 [d]1Jn 1:6; 2:11 **12:36** [e]ver 46; S Lk 16:8 [f]Jn 8:59 **12:37** [g]S Jn 2:11 **12:38** [h]Isa 53:1; Ro 10:16 **12:40** [i]Isa 6:10; S Mt 13:13,15 **12:41** [j]Isa 6:1-4 [k]Lk 24:27 **12:42** [l]ver 11; Jn 7:48 [m]S Jn 7:13 [n]Jn 9:22 **12:43** [o]1Sa 15:30 [p]S Ro 2:29 **12:44** [q]S Mt 10:40; Jn 5:24 **12:45** [r]S Jn 14:9 **12:46** [s]S Jn 1:4 **12:47** [t]S Jn 3:17 **12:48** [u]Jn 5:45 **12:49** [v]Jn 14:31 **12:50** [w]S Mt 25:46 [x]S Jn 14:24 **13:1** [y]S Jn 11:55 [z]S Mt 26:18 [a]Jn 16:28

[k] *34* Or *Messiah* [l] *38* Isaiah 53:1 [m] *40* Isaiah 6:10

such as Ps 89:36; 110:4; Isa 9:7; Da 7:14. *the Christ.* See note on 1:25. *Son of Man.* The only place in the Gospels where anyone other than Jesus used the expression, and even here Jesus is being quoted (see note on Mk 8:31).
**12:35–36** *the light.* Light is closely identified with Jesus, as seen from the call to believe in the light (see notes on 1:4; 8:12).
**12:37** *they still would not believe.* God's ancient people should have responded when God sent his Messiah. They should have seen the significance of the signs he did.
**12:39** *could not believe.* Does not mean that the people in question had no choice. They purposely rejected God and chose evil, and v. 40 explains that God in turn brought on them a judicial blinding of eyes and hardening of hearts. Yet many Jewish leaders did believe in Jesus as the Messiah (v. 42).
**12:40** These words from Isa 6:10 are quoted by Jesus (Mt 13:14–15; Mk 4:12; Lk 8:10) and by Paul (Ac 28:26–27).
**12:41** *saw Jesus' glory.* Isaiah spoke primarily of the glory of God (Isa 6:3). John spoke of the glory of Jesus and made no basic distinction between the two, attesting Jesus' oneness with God. The thought of glory here is complex. There is the idea of majesty, and there is also the idea (which meant so much to John) that Jesus' death on the cross and his subsequent resurrection and exaltation show his real glory. Isaiah foresaw the rejection of Christ, as the passages quoted (Isa 53:1; 6:10) show. He spoke of the Messiah both in the words about blind eyes and hard hearts, on the one hand, and about healing, on the other. This is the cross and this is glory, for the cross and resurrection and exaltation portray both suffering and healing, rejection and triumph, humiliation and glory.
**12:42** *many . . . leaders believed.* John does not give a picture of unrelieved gloom. Many Jewish leaders believed (see note on 1:7), though they remained secret believers for fear of excommunication (see note on 9:22).
**12:44** *cried out.* The words are given special emphasis by being spoken in a loud voice. *believe in me.* John ends his story of the public ministry of Jesus with an appeal for belief. He does not say when Jesus spoke these words (they may have been uttered earlier), but they are a fitting close to this part of his account. *the one who sent me.* Jesus' mission, as well as the inseparability of the Father and the Son, is stressed throughout this Gospel.
**12:46** *I have come into the world.* Points to both Jesus' preexistence and his mission. *light.* See notes on 1:4; 8:12.
**12:47** *to judge.* Not the purpose of Jesus' coming, but judgment is the other side of salvation. It is not the purpose of the sun's shining to cast shadows, but when the sun shines, shadows are inevitable.
**12:49** *the Father . . . commanded me what to say.* Jesus' hearers have a great responsibility. His "word" (v. 48) is that which the Father commanded him to say. To reject it, therefore, is to reject God.
**12:50** *eternal life.* See note on 3:15. *So.* Jesus said what he did in order to fulfill the will of the Father—a wonderful note on which to end the account of Jesus' public ministry.
**13:1–17:26** John has by far the longest account of the

who were in the world, he now showed
them the full extent of his love.[n]
2The evening meal was being served,
and the devil had already prompted Judas
Iscariot, son of Simon, to betray Jesus.[b]
3Jesus knew that the Father had put all
things under his power,[c] and that he had
come from God[d] and was returning to
God; 4so he got up from the meal, took off
his outer clothing, and wrapped a towel
around his waist.[e] 5After that, he poured
water into a basin and began to wash his
disciples' feet,[f] drying them with the towel that was wrapped around him.
6He came to Simon Peter, who said to
him, "Lord, are you going to wash my
feet?"
7Jesus replied, "You do not realize now
what I am doing, but later you will understand."[g]
8"No," said Peter, "you shall never
wash my feet."
Jesus answered, "Unless I wash you,
you have no part with me."
9"Then, Lord," Simon Peter replied,
"not just my feet but my hands and my
head as well!"
10Jesus answered, "A person who has
had a bath needs only to wash his feet; his
whole body is clean. And you are clean,[h]
though not every one of you."[i] 11For he
knew who was going to betray him,[j] and
that was why he said not every one was
clean.
12When he had finished washing their
feet, he put on his clothes and returned to
his place. "Do you understand what I have
done for you?" he asked them. 13"You call
me 'Teacher'[k] and 'Lord,'[l] and rightly so,
for that is what I am. 14Now that I, your
Lord and Teacher, have washed your feet,
you also should wash one another's feet.[m]
15I have set you an example that you
should do as I have done for you.[n] 16I tell
you the truth, no servant is greater than his
master,[o] nor is a messenger greater than
the one who sent him. 17Now that you
know these things, you will be blessed if
you do them.[p]

### *Jesus Predicts His Betrayal*

18"I am not referring to all of you;[q] I
know those I have chosen.[r] But this is to
fulfill the scripture:[s] 'He who shares my
bread[t] has lifted up his heel[u] against
me.'[o][v]
19"I am telling you now before it happens, so that when it does happen you will
believe[w] that I am He.[x] 20I tell you the

**13:2** [b]S Mt 10:4 **13:3** [c]S Mt 28:18 [d]Jn 8:42; 16:27, 28,30; 17:8 **13:4** [e]S Mt 20:28 **13:5** [f]S Lk 7:44 **13:7** [g]ver 12 **13:10** [h]Jn 15:3 [i]ver 18 **13:11** [j]S Mt 10:4 **13:13** [k]Mt 26:18; Jn 11:28 [l]S Mt 28:18; Lk 1:43; 2:11; 6:46; 11:1; Ac 10:36; Ro 10:9,12; 14:9; 1Co 12:3; Php 2:11; Col 2:6 **13:14** [m]1Pe 5:5 **13:15** [n]S Mt 11:29; S 1Ti 4:12 **13:16** [o]Mt 10:24; Lk 6:40; Jn 15:20 **13:17** [p]Mt 7:24, 25; Lk 11:28; Jas 1:25 **13:18** [q]ver 10 [r]Jn 15:16,19 [s]S Mt 1:22 [t]Mt 26:23 [u]Jn 6:70 [v]Ps 41:9 **13:19** [w]Jn 14:29; 16:4 [x]Jn 4:26; 8:24

[n] *1* Or *he loved them to the last* [o] *18* Psalm 41:9

---

upper room, though curiously he says nothing about the institution of the Lord's Supper. Still we owe to him most of our information about what our Lord said to his disciples on that night. One feature of the discourse is Jesus' emphasis on love. The word occurs only six times in chs. 1–12 but 31 times in chs. 13–17.

**13:1** *Passover Feast.* See notes on 2:13; 5:1. *the time.* See note on 2:4.

**13:2** *evening meal.* Some believe that this feast was a fellowship meal eaten sometime before the Passover Feast. This would mean that the Last Supper could not have been the Passover meal as the Synoptic Gospels clearly indicate. However, this meal may have been the Passover Feast itself, in which case the accounts of the Synoptics and John would agree. *the devil.* See v. 27. *Judas Iscariot.* See note on 6:71.

**13:3** *the Father had put all things under his power.* John again emphasizes the fulfillment of God's plan and Jesus' control of the situation.

**13:5** *began to wash his disciples' feet.* A menial task (see note on 1:27), normally performed by a servant. On this occasion there was no servant and no one else volunteered. Jesus' action was during the meal, not upon arrival, done deliberately to emphasize a point. It was a lesson in humility, but it also set forth the principle of selfless service that was so soon to be exemplified in the cross. John alone tells of this incident, but Luke says that in rebuking the disciples over a quarrel concerning who would be the greatest, Jesus said, "I am among you as one who serves" (Lk 22:27). Jesus' life of service would culminate on the cross.

**13:8** *No.* Characteristically, Peter objected, though apparently no one else did. He was a mixture of humility (he did not want Jesus to perform this lowly service for him) and pride (he tried to dictate to Jesus). *Unless I wash you.* Jesus' reply looks beyond the incident to what it symbolizes: Peter needed a spiritual cleansing. The external washing was a picture of cleansing from sin, which Christians also sometimes need (see note on 1Jn 1:9).

**13:9** *my hands and my head.* Peter's response was wholehearted, but he was still dictating to Jesus.

**13:10** *only to wash his feet.* A man would bathe himself before going to a feast. When he arrived, he only needed to wash his feet to be entirely clean again.

**13:11** *he knew.* Again John emphasizes Jesus' command of the situation.

**13:13** *Teacher . . . Lord.* An instructor would normally be called "Teacher," but "Lord" referred to one occupying the supreme place. Jesus accepted both titles.

**13:14–15** Some Christians believe that Christ intended to institute a foot-washing ordinance to be practiced regularly. Most Christians, however, interpret Christ's action here as providing an example of humble service.

**13:14** *wash one another's feet.* Christians should be willing to perform the most menial services for one another.

**13:16** With minor variations this saying, which Jesus used often, is found in 15:20; Mt 10:24; Lk 6:40 (cf. Lk 22:27).

**13:18** *not referring to all of you.* Jesus was leading up to his prediction of the betrayal (v. 21). *shares my bread.* To eat bread together was a mark of close fellowship (see note on Ps 41:9). *lifted up his heel.* May be derived from a horse's preparing to kick, or perhaps something like shaking off the dust from one's feet (Lk 9:5; 10:11).

**13:19** *so that . . . you will believe.* See 20:31. Jesus' concern was for the disciples, not himself. *I am He.* An emphatic form of speech, such as that in 8:58 (see note there).

**13:20** *anyone I send . . . the one who sent me.* Jesus' mission is a common theme in this Gospel, and now the mission of his followers is linked with it (cf. 20:21).

truth, whoever accepts anyone I send accepts me; and whoever accepts me accepts
the one who sent me."[y]
21After he had said this, Jesus was troubled in spirit[z] and testified, "I tell you the
truth, one of you is going to betray me."[a]
22His disciples stared at one another, at a
loss to know which of them he meant.
23One of them, the disciple whom Jesus
loved,[b] was reclining next to him. 24Simon
Peter motioned to this disciple and said,
"Ask him which one he means."
25Leaning back against Jesus, he asked
him, "Lord, who is it?"[c]
26Jesus answered, "It is the one to
whom I will give this piece of bread when
I have dipped it in the dish." Then, dipping
the piece of bread, he gave it to Judas Iscariot,[d] son of Simon. 27As soon as Judas
took the bread, Satan entered into him.[e]
"What you are about to do, do quickly,"
Jesus told him, 28but no one at the meal
understood why Jesus said this to him.
29Since Judas had charge of the money,[f]
some thought Jesus was telling him to buy
what was needed for the Feast,[g] or to give
something to the poor.[h] 30As soon as Judas
had taken the bread, he went out. And it
was night.[i]

### *Jesus Predicts Peter's Denial*

*13:37,38pp — Mt 26:33–35; Mk 14:29–31; Lk 22:33,34*

31When he was gone, Jesus said, "Now
is the Son of Man[j] glorified[k] and God is
glorified in him.[l] 32If God is glorified in
him,[p] God will glorify the Son in himself,[m]
and will glorify him at once.
33"My children, I will be with you only
a little longer. You will look for me, and
just as I told the Jews, so I tell you now:
Where I am going, you cannot come.[n]
34"A new command[o] I give you: Love
one another.[p] As I have loved you, so you
must love one another.[q] 35By this all men
will know that you are my disciples, if you
love one another."[r]
36Simon Peter asked him, "Lord, where
are you going?"[s]
Jesus replied, "Where I am going, you
cannot follow now,[t] but you will follow
later."[u]
37Peter asked, "Lord, why can't I follow
you now? I will lay down my life for you."
38Then Jesus answered, "Will you really
lay down your life for me? I tell you the
truth, before the rooster crows, you will
disown me three times![v]

### *Jesus Comforts His Disciples*

14 "Do not let your hearts be troubled.[w] Trust[x] in God[q];[y] trust also
in me. 2In my Father's house are many
rooms; if it were not so, I would have told
you. I am going there[z] to prepare a place
for you. 3And if I go and prepare a place for
you, I will come back[a] and take you to be

**13:20** [y]S Mt 10:40 **13:21** [z]S Jn 12:27 [a]Mt 26:21 **13:23** [b]Jn 19:26; 20:2; 21:7,20 **13:25** [c]Mt 26:22; Jn 21:20 **13:26** [d]S Mt 10:4 **13:27** [e]Lk 22:3 **13:29** [f]Jn 12:6 [g]ver 1 [h]Jn 12:5 **13:30** [i]Lk 22:53 **13:31** [j]S Mt 8:20 [k]Jn 7:39; 12:23 [l]Jn 14:13; 17:4; 1Pe 4:11 **13:32** [m]Jn 17:1 **13:33** [n]S Jn 7:33, 34 **13:34** [o]Jn 15:12; 1Jn 2:7-11; 3:11 [p]Lev 19:18; 1Th 4:9; 1Pe 1:22 [q]Jn 15:12; Eph 5:2; 1Jn 4:10, 11 **13:35** [r]1Jn 3:14; 4:20 **13:36** [s]Jn 16:5 [t]ver 33; Jn 14:2 [u]Jn 21:18,19; 2Pe 1:14 **13:38** [v]Jn 18:27 **14:1** [w]ver 27 [x]S Jn 3:15 [y]Ps 4:5 **14:2** [z]Jn 13:33, 36; 16:5 **14:3** [a]ver 18,28; S Mt 16:27

[p]*32* Many early manuscripts do not have *If God is glorified in him.* [q]*1* Or *You trust in God*

---

**13:21** *troubled.* See 11:33. Though he knew of it long before it happened, Jesus was grieved by the betrayal of a friend.
**13:22** *at a loss.* The disciples' astonishment shows that Judas had concealed his contacts with the high priests. No one suspected him (see v. 28), but all seem to have thought that the betrayal would be involuntary (see Mk 14:19).
**13:23** *the disciple whom Jesus loved.* Usually thought to be John, the author of this Gospel (see 19:26; 20:2; 21:7, 20). The expression does not, of course, mean that Jesus did not love the others, but that there was a special bond with this man. *reclining.* At a dinner, guests reclined on couches, leaning on the left elbow with the head toward the table.
**13:26** *the one to whom I . . . give . . . bread . . . dipped . . . in the dish.* Evidently Judas was near Jesus, possibly in the seat of honor. John used Judas's full name (see note on 6:71) in recording this solemn moment.
**13:27** *As soon as Judas took the bread.* Evidently the critical moment. If the giving of the bread to Judas was a mark of honor, it also seems to have been a final appeal—which Judas did not accept. *Satan.* The name is used only here in John (cf. v. 2). *do quickly.* Jesus' words once more indicate his control. He would die as he directed, not as his opponents determined.
**13:29** *the Feast.* See v. 1 and note on v. 2. *the poor.* See 12:5.
**13:30** *night.* In light of John's emphasis on the conflict between light and darkness, this may have been more than a time note—picturing also the darkness of Judas's soul.
**13:31** *Son of Man.* See note on Mk 8:31. *glorified.* See v. 32 and note on 7:39. Here the idea of glory includes a reference to Jesus' sacrificial death on the cross and the glorious salvation that would result. *God is glorified in him.* The glory of the Father is closely bound to that of the Son.
**13:34** *A new command.* In a sense it was an old one (see Lev 19:18), but for Christ's disciples it was new, because it was the mark of their brotherhood, created by Christ's great love for them (cf. Mt 22:37–39; Mk 12:30–31; Lk 10:27). *As I have loved you.* Our standard is Christ's love for us.
**13:35** *love.* The distinguishing mark of Christ's followers (cf. 1Jn 3:23; 4:7–8,11–12,19–21).
**13:36** *where are you going?* Peter seems to have ignored Jesus' words about love and was more concerned about his Master's departure. In Jesus' reply "you" is singular and thus personal to Peter, whereas in v. 33 the word is plural.
**13:37** *I will lay down my life.* Words similar to those of the good shepherd in 10:11. Peter was characteristically sure of himself, when in fact he would not at this time lay down his life for Jesus. Exactly the opposite would be true.
**13:38** *you will disown me three times.* Peter's denial is prophesied in all four Gospels (Mt 26:33–35; Mk 14:29–31; Lk 22:31–34).
**14:1** *Do not . . . be troubled.* The apostles had just received disturbing news (13:33,36). *Trust.* The antidote for a troubled heart.
**14:2** *my Father's house.* Heaven. *rooms.* Lit. "dwelling places," implying permanence.
**14:3** *I will come back.* Jesus comes in many ways, but the

with me that you also may be where I
am.[b] 4You know the way to the place
where I am going."

## *Jesus the Way to the Father*

5Thomas[c] said to him, "Lord, we don't
know where you are going, so how can we
know the way?"
6Jesus answered, "I am[d] the way[e] and
the truth[f] and the life.[g] No one comes to
the Father except through me.[h] 7If you
really knew me, you would know[r] my Father as well.[i] From now on, you do know
him and have seen him."
8Philip[j] said, "Lord, show us the Father
and that will be enough for us."
9Jesus answered: "Don't you know me,
Philip, even after I have been among you
such a long time? Anyone who has seen
me has seen the Father.[k] How can you
say, 'Show us the Father'? 10Don't you believe that I am in the Father, and that the
Father is in me?[l] The words I say to you
are not just my own.[m] Rather, it is the
Father, living in me, who is doing his
work. 11Believe me when I say that I am in
the Father and the Father is in me; or at
least believe on the evidence of the miracles themselves.[n] 12I tell you the truth,
anyone who has faith[o] in me will do what
I have been doing.[p] He will do even
greater things than these, because I am going to the Father. 13And I will do whatever
you ask[q] in my name, so that the Son may
bring glory to the Father. 14You may ask
me for anything in my name, and I will do
it.

## *Jesus Promises the Holy Spirit*

15"If you love me, you will obey what I
command.[r] 16And I will ask the Father,
and he will give you another Counselor[s]
to be with you forever— 17the Spirit of
truth.[t] The world cannot accept him,[u]
because it neither sees him nor knows
him. But you know him, for he lives with
you and will be[s] in you. 18I will not leave
you as orphans;[v] I will come to you.[w]
19Before long, the world will not see me
anymore, but you will see me.[x] Because I
live, you also will live.[y] 20On that day[z]
you will realize that I am in my Father,[a]
and you are in me, and I am in you.[b]
21Whoever has my commands and obeys
them, he is the one who loves me.[c] He
who loves me will be loved by my Father,[d] and I too will love him and show
myself to him."
22Then Judas[e] (not Judas Iscariot) said,
"But, Lord, why do you intend to show
yourself to us and not to the world?"[f]
23Jesus replied, "If anyone loves me, he

**14:3** [b]S Jn 12:26 **14:5** [c]S Jn 11:16 **14:6** [d]S Jn 6:35 [e]Jn 10:9; Eph 2:18; Heb 10:20 [f]Jn 1:14 [g]S Jn 1:4 [h]Ac 4:12 **14:7** [i]Jn 1:18; S 1Jn 2:23 **14:8** [j]S Jn 1:43 **14:9** [k]Isa 9:6; Jn 1:14; 12:45; 2Co 4:4; Php 2:6; Col 1:15; Heb 1:3 **14:10** [l]ver 11,20; Jn 10:38; 17:21 [m]S ver 24 **14:11** [n]Jn 5:36; 10:38 **14:12** [o]Mt 21:21 [p]Lk 10:17 **14:13** [q]S Mt 7:7 **14:15** [r]ver 21,23; Ps 103:18; Jn 15:10; 1Jn 2:3-5; 3:22, 24; 5:3; 2Jn 6; Rev 12:17; 14:12 **14:16** [s]ver 26; Jn 15:26; 16:7 **14:17** [t]Jn 15:26; 16:13; 1Jn 4:6; 5:6 [u]1Co 2:14 **14:18** [v]1Ki 6:13 [w]ver 3,28; S Mt 16:27 **14:19** [x]Jn 7:33, 34; 16:16 [y]Jn 6:57 **14:20** [z]Jn 16:23, 26 [a]ver 10,11; Jn 10:38; 17:21 [b]S Ro 8:10 **14:21** [c]S ver 15 [d]Dt 7:13; Jn 16:27; 1Jn 2:5 **14:22** [e]Lk 6:16; Ac 1:13 [f]Ac 10:41

[r]7 Some early manuscripts *If you really have known me, you will know* [s]17 Some early manuscripts *and is*

---

primary reference here is to his second advent.
**14:4** *way.* See v. 6.
**14:5** *Thomas.* He was honest, and plainly told the Lord he did not understand (see note on 11:16).
**14:6** *I am.* See note on 6:35. *the way.* To God. Jesus is not one way among many, but the way (cf. Ac 4:12; Heb 10:19–20). In the early church, Christianity was sometimes called "the Way" (e.g., Ac 9:2; 19:9,23). *the truth.* A key emphasis in this Gospel (see note on 1:14). *the life.* See note on 1:4. Very likely the statement means "I am the way (to the Father) in that I am the truth and the life."
**14:7** *me . . . my Father.* Once more Jesus stresses the intimate connection between the Father and himself. Jesus brought a full revelation of the Father (cf. 1:18), so that the apostles had real knowledge of him.
**14:10** *not just my own.* Jesus' teaching was not of human origin, and there was an inseparable connection between his words and his work.
**14:11** *Believe . . . that I am in the Father and the Father is in me.* Saving faith is trust in a person, but it must also have factual content. Faith includes believing that Jesus is one with the Father.
**14:12** *greater things.* Miracles (see v. 11). These depended on Jesus' going to the Father, because they are works done in the strength of the Holy Spirit, whom Jesus would send from the Father (15:26; cf. 14:16–17).
**14:13** *in my name.* Not simply prayer that mentions Jesus' name but prayer in accordance with all that the person who bears the name is (see note on 2:23). It is prayer aimed at carrying forward the work Jesus did—prayer that he himself will answer (see also v. 14).
**14:15** *love . . . obey.* Love, like faith (Jas 2:14–26), cannot be separated from obedience.
**14:16** *the Father . . . will give you.* The first of a series of important passages about the Holy Spirit (v. 26; 15:26; 16:7–15), the gift of the Father. *another.* Besides Jesus. *Counselor.* Or "Helper." It is a legal term, but with a broader meaning than "counsel for the defense" (see 1Jn 2:1). It referred to any person who helped someone in trouble with the law. The Spirit will always stand by Christ's people.
**14:17** *the Spirit of truth.* In essence and in action the Spirit is characterized by truth. He brings people to the truth of God. All three persons of the Trinity are linked with truth. See also the Father (4:23–24; cf. Ps 31:5; Isa 65:16) and the Son (14:6). *The world.* Which takes no notice of the Spirit of God (cf. 1Co 2:14). But the Spirit was "with" Jesus' disciples and would be "in" them. Some believe the latter relationship (indwelling) specifically anticipates the coming of the Holy Spirit on the day of Pentecost (Ac 2; cf. Ro 8:9).
**14:18** *I will come to you.* The words relate to the coming of the Spirit, but Jesus also speaks of his own appearances after the resurrection and at his second coming (see vv. 3, 19, 28; 16:22).
**14:19** *the world . . . but you.* The cross separated the world (who would not see Jesus thereafter) from the disciples (who would). *Because I live, you also will live.* The life of the Christian always depends on the life of Christ (cf. 1:4; 3:15).
**14:20** *On that day you will realize.* The resurrection would radically change their thinking.
**14:21** *obeys . . . loves.* Love for Christ and keeping his commands cannot be separated (see note on v. 15). *loved by my Father . . . I too will love him.* The love of the Father cannot be separated from that of the Son.
**14:22** *why . . . ?* He (and, for that matter, the others)

will obey my teaching.[g] My Father will
love him, and we will come to him and
make our home with him.[h] 24He who
does not love me will not obey my teaching. These words you hear are not my
own; they belong to the Father who sent
me.
25"All this I have spoken while still with
you. 26But the Counselor,[i] the Holy Spirit,
whom the Father will send in my name,[k]
will teach you all things[l] and will remind
you of everything I have said to you.[m]
27Peace I leave with you; my peace I give
you.[n] I do not give to you as the world
gives. Do not let your hearts be troubled[o]
and do not be afraid.
28"You heard me say, 'I am going away
and I am coming back to you.'[p] If you
loved me, you would be glad that I am
going to the Father,[q] for the Father is
greater than I.[r] 29I have told you now before it happens, so that when it does happen you will believe.[s] 30I will not speak
with you much longer, for the prince of
this world[t] is coming. He has no hold on
me, 31but the world must learn that I love
the Father and that I do exactly what my
Father has commanded me.[u]
"Come now; let us leave.

**14:23** [g]S ver 15 [h]S Ro 8:10 **14:24** [i]ver 10; Dt 18:18; Jn 5:19; 7:16; 8:28; 12:49,50 **14:26** [j]ver 16; Jn 15:26; 16:7 [k]Ac 2:33 [l]Jn 16:13; 1Jn 2:20,27 [m]Jn 2:22 **14:27** [n]Nu 6:26; Ps 85:8; Mal 2:6; S Lk 2:14; 24:36; Jn 16:33; Php 4:7; Col 3:15 [o]ver 1 **14:28** [p]ver 2-4, 18; S Mt 16:27 [q]Jn 5:18 [r]Jn 10:29 **14:29** [s]Jn 13:19; 16:4 **14:30** [t]S Jn 12:31 **14:31** [u]Jn 10:18; 12:49

**15:1** [v]S Jn 6:35 [w]Ps 80:8-11; Isa 5:1-7 **15:2** [x]ver 6; S Mt 3:10 [y]Ps 92:14; Mt 3:8; 7:20; Gal 5:22; Eph 5:9; Php 1:11 **15:3** [z]Jn 13:10; 17:17; Eph 5:26 **15:4** [a]S Jn 6:56 **15:5** [b]ver 16 **15:6** [c]ver 2; Eze 15:4; S Mt 3:10 **15:7** [d]ver 4; S Jn 6:56 [e]S Mt 7:7

## *The Vine and the Branches*

15 "I am[v] the true vine,[w] and my Father is the gardener. 2He cuts off
every branch in me that bears no fruit,[x]
while every branch that does bear fruit[y]
he prunes[t] so that it will be even more
fruitful. 3You are already clean because of
the word I have spoken to you.[z] 4Remain
in me, and I will remain in you.[a] No
branch can bear fruit by itself; it must remain in the vine. Neither can you bear
fruit unless you remain in me.
5"I am the vine; you are the branches. If
a man remains in me and I in him, he will
bear much fruit;[b] apart from me you can
do nothing. 6If anyone does not remain in
me, he is like a branch that is thrown away
and withers; such branches are picked up,
thrown into the fire and burned.[c] 7If you
remain in me[d] and my words remain in
you, ask whatever you wish, and it will be
given you.[e] 8This is to my Father's glory,[f]
that you bear much fruit, showing yourselves to be my disciples.[g]
9"As the Father has loved me,[h] so have
I loved you. Now remain in my love. 10If

**15:8** [f]S Mt 9:8 [g]Jn 8:31 **15:9** [h]Jn 17:23,24,26

[t]2 The Greek for *prunes* also means *cleans.*

---

probably looked for Jesus to fulfill popular Messianic expectations. It was not easy, therefore, to understand how that would mean showing himself to the disciples but not to the world.

**14:23** *loves . . . obey . . . love.* Again love and obedience are linked (cf. vv. 15,21).

**14:24** Once more the close relationship between Jesus' words and the Father's is stressed (see v. 10; 7:16).

**14:26** *Counselor.* See note on v. 16. *Holy Spirit.* His normal title in the NT (though only here and at 1:33 in this Gospel)—emphasizing his holiness, rather than his power or greatness. *whom the Father will send.* Both the Father and the Son are involved in the sending (see 15:26). *name.* See notes on v. 13; 2:23. *remind you of everything I have said to you.* Crucial for the life of the church—and for the writing of the NT.

**14:27** *Peace . . . my peace.* A common Hebrew greeting (20:19,21,26), which Jesus uses here in an unusual way. The term speaks, in effect, of the salvation that Christ's redemptive work will achieve for his disciples—total well-being and inner rest of spirit, in fellowship with God. All true peace is his gift, which the repetition emphasizes. *I do not give . . . as the world gives.* In its greetings of peace the world can only express a longing or wish. But Jesus' peace is real and present. *troubled.* See note on v. 1.

**14:28** *heard me say.* Cf. v. 3. *the Father is greater than I.* Revealing the subordinate role Jesus accepted as a necessary part of the incarnation. The statement must be understood in the light of the unity between the Father and the Son (10:30).

**14:30** *prince of this world.* See note on 12:31. *has no hold on me.* Satan has a hold on people because of their fallen state. Since Christ was sinless, Satan could have no hold on him.

**14:31** *I do exactly what my Father has commanded me.* Jesus had stressed the importance of his followers being obedient (vv. 15,21,23), and he set the example. With these words he goes to fulfill his mission (chs. 18–19).

**15:1** *I am.* See note on 6:35. *the true vine.* The vine is frequently used in the OT as a symbol of Israel (e.g., Ps 80:8–16; Isa 5:1–7; Jer 2:21). When this imagery is used, Israel is often shown as lacking in some way. Jesus, however, is "the true vine."

**15:2** *cuts off.* A reference to judgment (see note on v. 6). *prunes.* Pruning produces fruitfulness. In the NT the figure of good fruit represents the product of a godly life (see Mt 3:8; 7:16–20) or virtues of character (see Gal 5:22–23; Eph 5:9; Php 1:11).

**15:3** *clean.* See NIV text note on v. 2. *the word.* Sums up the message of Jesus.

**15:4** *Remain in me.* The believer has no fruitfulness apart from his union and fellowship with Christ. A branch out of contact with the vine is lifeless.

**15:5** *I am the vine.* See note on v. 1. The repetition gives emphasis. *remains in me and I in him.* A living union with Christ is absolutely necessary; without it there is nothing.

**15:6** *thrown into the fire and burned.* Judged (see note on v. 2). In light of such passages as 6:39; 10:27–28, these branches probably do not represent true believers. Genuine salvation is evidenced by a life of fruitfulness (see v. 10 and notes on vv. 2,4; see also Heb 6:9, "things that accompany salvation").

**15:7** *my words remain in you.* It is impossible to pray correctly apart from knowing and believing the teachings of Christ. *ask whatever you wish.* See 14:13 and note.

**15:8** *to my Father's glory.* The Father is glorified in the work of the Son (13:31–32), and he is also glorified in the fruit-bearing of disciples (see Mt 7:20; Lk 6:43–45).

**15:10** *obey . . . as I have obeyed.* Again the importance of obedience (cf. 14:15,21,23), and again the example of Christ

you obey my commands,[i] you will remain
in my love, just as I have obeyed my Father's commands and remain in his love.
11I have told you this so that my joy may
be in you and that your joy may be complete.[j] 12My command is this: Love each
other as I have loved you.[k] 13Greater love
has no one than this, that he lay down his
life for his friends.[l] 14You are my friends[m]
if you do what I command.[n] 15I no longer
call you servants, because a servant does
not know his master's business. Instead, I
have called you friends, for everything that
I learned from my Father I have made
known to you.[o] 16You did not choose me,
but I chose you and appointed you[p] to go
and bear fruit[q]—fruit that will last. Then
the Father will give you whatever you ask
in my name.[r] 17This is my command:
Love each other.[s]

## *The World Hates the Disciples*

18"If the world hates you,[t] keep in
mind that it hated me first. 19If you belonged to the world, it would love you as
its own. As it is, you do not belong to the
world, but I have chosen you[u] out of the
world. That is why the world hates you.[v]
20Remember the words I spoke to you: 'No
servant is greater than his master.'[u][w] If
they persecuted me, they will persecute
you also.[x] If they obeyed my teaching,
they will obey yours also. 21They will treat
you this way because of my name,[y] for
they do not know the One who sent me.[z]
22If I had not come and spoken to them,[a]
they would not be guilty of sin. Now, however, they have no excuse for their sin.[b]
23He who hates me hates my Father as
well. 24If I had not done among them what
no one else did,[c] they would not be guilty
of sin.[d] But now they have seen these
miracles, and yet they have hated both me
and my Father. 25But this is to fulfill what
is written in their Law:[e] 'They hated me
without reason.'[v][f]

26"When the Counselor[g] comes, whom
I will send to you from the Father,[h] the
Spirit of truth[i] who goes out from the Father, he will testify about me.[j] 27And you
also must testify,[k] for you have been with
me from the beginning.[l]

16 "All this[m] I have told you so that
you will not go astray.[n] 2They will
put you out of the synagogue;[o] in fact, a
time is coming when anyone who kills you
will think he is offering a service to God.[p]
3They will do such things because they
have not known the Father or me.[q] 4I
have told you this, so that when the time
comes you will remember[r] that I warned

**15:10** [i]S Jn 14:15 **15:11** [j]S Jn 3:29 **15:12** [k]ver 17; S Jn 13:34 **15:13** [l]Ge 44:33; Jn 10:11; Ro 5:7, 8 **15:14** [m]Job 16:20; Pr 18:24; Lk 12:4 [n]Mt 12:50 **15:15** [o]Jn 8:26 **15:16** [p]ver 19; Jn 13:18 [q]ver 5 [r]S Mt 7:7 **15:17** [s]ver 12 **15:18** [t]Isa 66:5; Jn 7:7; 1Jn 3:13 **15:19** [u]ver 16 [v]Jn 17:14 **15:20** [w]S Jn 13:16 [x]2Ti 3:12 **15:21** [y]Isa 66:5; Mt 5:10,11; 10:22; Lk 6:22; Ac 5:41; 1Pe 4:14; Rev 2:3 [z]Jn 16:3 **15:22** [a]Eze 2:5; 3:7 [b]Jn 9:41; Ro 1:20; 2:1 **15:24** [c]Jn 5:36 [d]Jn 9:41 **15:25** [e]S Jn 10:34 [f]Ps 35:19; 69:4; 109:3 **15:26** [g]Jn 14:16 [h]Jn 14:26; 16:7 [i]S Jn 14:17 [j]1Jn 5:7 **15:27** [k]S Lk 24:48; Jn 21:24; 1Jn 1:2; 4:14 [l]S Lk 1:2 **16:1** [m]Jn 15:18-27 [n]Mt 11:6 **16:2** [o]Jn 9:22; 12:42 [p]Isa 66:5; Ac 26:9,10; Rev 6:9 **16:3** [q]Jn 15:21; 17:25; 1Jn 3:1 **16:4** [r]Jn 13:19; 14:29

[u]*20* John 13:16 [v]*25* Psalms 35:19; 69:4

(cf. 14:31). *my love . . . his love.* See vv. 12,14. Obedience and love go together (see 1Jn 2:5; 5:2–3).

**15:11** *joy.* Mentioned previously in this Gospel only in 3:29, but one of the characteristic notes of the upper room discourse (16:20–22,24; 17:13). The Christian way is never dreary, for Jesus desires his disciples' joy to be complete.

**15:13** Christ's love was not only in words but also in his sacrificial death.

**15:15** *servants . . . friends.* A servant is simply an agent, doing what his master commands and often not understanding his master's purpose. But Jesus takes his friends into his confidence. *everything . . . I have made known to you.* From 16:12 we learn that though Jesus had let his disciples know as much as they were able to absorb of the Father's plan, the revelation was not yet complete. The Spirit would make other things known in due course.

**15:16** *I chose you . . . bear fruit . . . ask.* Disciples normally chose the particular rabbi to whom they wanted to be attached, but it was not so with Jesus' disciples. He chose them, and for a purpose—the bearing of fruit. We usually desire a strong prayer life in order that we may be fruitful, but here it is the other way around. Jesus enables us to bear fruit, and then the Father will hear our prayers. *name.* See notes on 2:23; 14:13.

**15:18–19** *world.* Here refers to the human system that opposes God's purpose (see note on 1:10).

**15:19** *you do not belong.* The believer's essential being, his new life, comes specially from God, and therefore he is not the same as those who oppose God.

**15:21** *They will treat you this way.* Because Christians do not belong to the world, persecution from the world is inevitable. The basic reason is the world's ignorance and rejection of the Father (cf. 16:3). *name.* See note on 2:23.

**15:22** *no excuse.* Privilege and responsibility go together. The Jews had had the great privilege of having the Son of God among them—in addition to having received God's special revelation in the OT. Their rejection of Jesus left them totally guilty and without excuse. Had he not come to them they would still have been sinners, but they would not have been guilty of rejecting him directly (see v. 24).

**15:25** *to fulfill what is written.* In the end God's purpose is always accomplished, despite the belief of sinful men that they have successfully opposed it. *Law.* See notes on 10:34; 12:34.

**15:26** *Counselor.* See note on 14:16. *I will send.* See notes on 14:16,26. *Spirit of truth.* See note on 14:17. *goes out from the Father.* Probably refers to the Spirit's being sent to do the Father's work on earth rather than to his eternal relationship with the Father. *testify.* See note on 1:7.

**15:27** *you also.* Emphatic. Believers bear their testimony to Christ in the power of the Spirit. But it is their testimony, and they are responsible for bearing it. *from the beginning.* The apostles bore the definitive testimony, for they were uniquely chosen and taught by Christ and were eyewitnesses of his glory (see Lk 24:48; Ac 10:39,41).

**16:2** *put you out of the synagogue.* See note on 9:22. *a service to God.* Religious people have often persecuted others in the strong conviction that this was right (see Ac 26:9–11; Gal 1:13–14).

**16:3** *the Father.* See note on 5:17. *or me.* Again the Father and the Son are linked. Not to know Christ is to be ignorant of the Father.

you. I did not tell you this at first because I was with you.[s]

### *The Work of the Holy Spirit*

5"Now I am going to him who sent me,[t] yet none of you asks me, 'Where are you going?'[u] 6Because I have said these things, you are filled with grief.[v] 7But I tell you the truth: It is for your good that I am going away. Unless I go away, the Counselor[w] will not come to you; but if I go, I will send him to you.[x] 8When he comes, he will convict the world of guilt[w] in regard to sin and righteousness and judgment: 9in regard to sin,[y] because men do not believe in me; 10in regard to righteousness,[z] because I am going to the Father,[a] where you can see me no longer; 11and in regard to judgment, because the prince of this world[b] now stands condemned.

12"I have much more to say to you, more than you can now bear.[c] 13But when he, the Spirit of truth,[d] comes, he will guide you into all truth.[e] He will not speak on his own; he will speak only what he hears, and he will tell you what is yet to come. 14He will bring glory to me by taking from what is mine and making it known to you. 15All that belongs to the Father is mine.[f] That is why I said the Spirit will take from what is mine and make it known to you.

16"In a little while[g] you will see me no more, and then after a little while you will see me."[h]

### *The Disciples' Grief Will Turn to Joy*

17Some of his disciples said to one another, "What does he mean by saying, 'In a little while you will see me no more, and then after a little while you will see me,'[i] and 'Because I am going to the Father'?"[j] 18They kept asking, "What does he mean by 'a little while'? We don't understand what he is saying."

19Jesus saw that they wanted to ask him about this, so he said to them, "Are you asking one another what I meant when I said, 'In a little while you will see me no more, and then after a little while you will see me'? 20I tell you the truth, you will weep and mourn[k] while the world rejoices. You will grieve, but your grief will turn to joy.[l] 21A woman giving birth to a child has pain[m] because her time has come; but when her baby is born she forgets the anguish because of her joy that a child is born into the world. 22So with you: Now is your time of grief,[n] but I will see you again[o] and you will rejoice, and no

**16:4** [s]Jn 15:27 **16:5** [t]ver 10,17, 28; Jn 7:33 [u]Jn 13:36; 14:5 **16:6** [v]ver 22 **16:7** [w]Jn 14:16, 26; 15:26 [x]Jn 7:39; 14:26 **16:9** [y]Jn 15:22 **16:10** [z]Ac 3:14; 7:52; Ro 1:17; 3:21,22; 1Pe 3:18 [a]S ver 5 **16:11** [b]S Jn 12:31 **16:12** [c]Mk 4:33; 1Co 3:2 **16:13** [d]S Jn 14:17 [e]Ps 25:5; Jn 14:26 **16:15** [f]Jn 17:10 **16:16** [g]S Jn 7:33 [h]ver 22; Jn 14:18-24 **16:17** [i]ver 16 [j]ver 5 **16:20** [k]Mk 16:10; Lk 23:27 [l]Jn 20:20 **16:21** [m]Isa 13:8; 21:3; 26:17; Mic 4:9; 1Th 5:3 **16:22** [n]ver 6 [o]ver 16

**w**8 Or *will expose the guilt of the world*

---

**16:5** *none of you asks me, 'Where are you going?'* Peter had asked such a question (13:36), but quickly turned his attention to another subject. His concern had been with what would happen to himself and the others and not for where Jesus was going.
**16:6** *you are filled with grief.* Because of his announced departure.
**16:7** *Unless I go away.* Jesus did not say why the Spirit would not come until he went away, but clearly taught that his saving work on the cross was necessary before the sending of the Spirit. *Counselor.* See note on 14:16. *I will send him.* See note on 14:26.
**16:8** *he will convict the world.* The work the Spirit does in the world (see NIV text note). The NT normally speaks of his work in believers.
**16:9** *in regard to sin.* Apart from the Spirit's convicting work, people can never see themselves as sinners. *because men do not believe.* May mean that their sin is their failure to believe, or that their unbelief is a classic example of sin. Typically, John may have had both of these in mind.
**16:10** *in regard to righteousness.* The righteousness brought about by Christ's sacrificial death (cf. Ro 1:17; 3:21–22). No one but the Holy Spirit can reveal to a person that a righteous status before God does not depend on good works but on Christ's death on the cross. *because I am going to the Father.* The ascension, which as part of Christ's exaltation placed God's seal of approval on Christ's redemptive act.
**16:11** *in regard to judgment.* Jesus was speaking of the defeat of Satan, which was a form of judgment, not simply a victory. More than power is in question. God acts with justice. *prince of this world.* See note on 12:31.
**16:12** *more than you can now bear.* This may mean "more than you can understand now," or "more than you can perform without the Spirit's help" (to live out Christ's teaching requires the enabling presence of the Spirit).
**16:13** *Spirit of truth.* See note on 14:17. *only what he hears.* We are not told whether he hears from the Father or the Son, but it obviously does not matter, for the verse stresses the close relationship among the three. *what is yet to come.* Probably means the whole Christian way or revelation (presented and preserved in the apostolic writings), still future at the time Jesus spoke.
**16:14** *glory to me.* See note on 1:14. The Spirit draws no attention to himself but promotes the glory of Christ.
**16:15** *All that belongs to the Father is mine.* Cf. 17:10. The three Persons are closely related.
**16:16** *a little while . . . a little while.* Few doubt that the first phrase refers to the interval before the crucifixion. But interpretations differ as to whether the second refers to the interval preceding the resurrection or the coming of the Spirit or the second coming of Christ. It seems that the language here best fits the resurrection.
**16:17** *going to the Father.* See v. 10. Jesus had not linked this with "a little while," but the apostles saw them as connected.
**16:20** *weep.* The same verb for loud wailing as in 11:33, which carries the idea of deep sorrow and its outward expression.
**16:21** *A woman giving birth.* Giving birth usually causes both pain and joy (cf. Isa 26:17–19; 66:7–14; Hos 13:13–14).
**16:22** *I will see you again.* As in v. 16, probably a reference to Jesus' appearances after his resurrection. *no one will take away your joy.* The resurrection would change things permanently, bringing a joy that cannot be removed by the world's assaults.

one will take away your joy.[p] 23In that day[q] you will no longer ask me anything. I tell you the truth, my Father will give you whatever you ask in my name.[r] 24Until now you have not asked for anything in my name. Ask and you will receive,[s] and your joy will be complete.[t]

25"Though I have been speaking figuratively,[u] a time is coming[v] when I will no longer use this kind of language but will tell you plainly about my Father. 26In that day you will ask in my name.[w] I am not saying that I will ask the Father on your behalf. 27No, the Father himself loves you because you have loved me[x] and have believed that I came from God.[y] 28I came from the Father and entered the world; now I am leaving the world and going back to the Father."[z]

29Then Jesus' disciples said, "Now you are speaking clearly and without figures of speech.[a] 30Now we can see that you know all things and that you do not even need to have anyone ask you questions. This makes us believe[b] that you came from God."[c]

31"You believe at last!"[x] Jesus answered. 32"But a time is coming,[d] and has come, when you will be scattered,[e] each to his own home. You will leave me all alone.[f] Yet I am not alone, for my Father is with me.[g]

**16:22** [p]ver 20; Jer 31:12
**16:23** [q]ver 26; Jn 14:20 [r]S Mt 7:7
**16:24** [s]S Mt 7:7 [t]S Jn 3:29
**16:25** [u]ver 29; Ps 78:2; Eze 20:49; Mt 13:34; Mk 4:33,34; Jn 10:6 [v]ver 2
**16:26** [w]ver 23,24
**16:27** [x]Jn 14:21, 23 [y]ver 30; S Jn 13:3
**16:28** [z]ver 5,10, 17; Jn 13:3
**16:29** [a]S ver 25
**16:30** [b]1Ki 17:24 [c]ver 27; S Jn 13:3
**16:32** [d]ver 2,25 [e]Mt 26:31 [f]Mt 26:56 [g]Jn 8:16,29
**16:33** [h]S Jn 14:27 [i]Jn 15:18-21 [j]Ro 8:37; 1Jn 4:4; 5:4; Rev 2:7,11, 17,26; 3:5,12,21; 21:7
**17:1** [k]Jn 11:41 [l]S Mt 26:18 [m]Jn 12:23; 13:31,32
**17:2** [n]S Mt 28:18 [o]S Mt 25:46 [p]ver 6,9,24; Da 7:14; Jn 6:37,39
**17:3** [q]S Php 3:8 [r]ver 8,18,21,23, 25; S Jn 3:17
**17:4** [s]Jn 13:31 [t]S Jn 19:30
**17:5** [u]ver 1 [v]Php 2:6 [w]S Jn 1:2

33"I have told you these things, so that in me you may have peace.[h] In this world you will have trouble.[i] But take heart! I have overcome[j] the world."

## *Jesus Prays for Himself*

17 After Jesus said this, he looked toward heaven[k] and prayed:

"Father, the time has come.[l] Glorify your Son, that your Son may glorify you.[m] 2For you granted him authority over all people[n] that he might give eternal life[o] to all those you have given him.[p] 3Now this is eternal life: that they may know you,[q] the only true God, and Jesus Christ, whom you have sent.[r] 4I have brought you glory[s] on earth by completing the work you gave me to do.[t] 5And now, Father, glorify me[u] in your presence with the glory I had with you[v] before the world began.[w]

## *Jesus Prays for His Disciples*

6"I have revealed you[y][x] to those whom you gave me[y] out of the world. They were yours; you gave them to me and they have obeyed your word.

**17:6** [x]ver 26; Jn 1:18 [y]S ver 2

[x] *31* Or *"Do you now believe?"* [y] *6* Greek *your name;* also in verse 26

**16:23** *you will no longer ask me anything.* Seems to mean asking for information (rather than asking in prayer), which would not be necessary after the resurrection. Jesus then moved on to the subject of prayer. However, Jesus may have been saying that his disciples previously had been praying to Christ, but after his death and resurrection they were to go directly to the Father and pray in Christ's name (see vv. 24,26–27 and notes). *name.* See notes on 2:23; 14:13.
**16:24** *Until now.* Previously they had asked the Father or Christ, but they had not asked the Father in Christ's name. *your joy.* See note on 15:11.
**16:25** *I have been speaking figuratively.* Throughout the discourse, not just in the immediately preceding words. *a time is coming.* After the resurrection.
**16:26** *in my name.* See notes on 2:23; 14:13. *I am not saying that I will ask.* Not a contradiction of Ro 8:34; Heb 7:25; 1Jn 2:1. Those passages mean that Christ's presence in heaven as the crucified and risen Lord is itself an intercession. Here the teaching is that there will be no need for him to make petitions in our behalf.
**16:27** *the Father himself loves you.* Christ is explaining why the disciples can come directly to the Father in prayer. It is because the disciples have loved and trusted in Jesus, and in love God will hear their requests in Jesus' name.
**16:29** *without figures of speech.* See v. 25 and note.
**16:30** *believe that you came from God.* Two recurring themes of this Gospel: believing (see note on 1:7) and Jesus' coming from God (see notes on 4:34; 17:3,8).
**16:32** *you will be scattered.* The disciples had faith, but not enough to stand firm in face of disaster. Jesus knew they would fail; however, his church is not built on people's strength but on God's ability to use people even after they have failed.
**16:33** Notice the contrasts: between "in me" and "in this world" (see note on 1:10) and between "peace" and "trouble." *I have overcome.* Just before his death Jesus affirms his final victory.
**17:1–26** Jesus' longest recorded prayer.
**17:1** *he looked toward heaven.* The customary attitude in prayer (11:41; Ps 123:1; Mk 7:34), though sometimes the person prostrated himself (see Mt 26:39). *Father.* Used of God in John's Gospel 122 times. *the time.* See note on 2:4. *Glorify . . . glorify.* See notes on 1:14; 7:39; 13:31. The glory of the Father and that of the Son are closely connected, and the death by which Jesus would glorify God would lead to eternal life for believers (v. 2).
**17:2** *granted.* The thought of giving is stressed in this chapter (vv. 4,6–9,11–12,14,22,24); see note on 3:27. *that he might give eternal life.* See note on 3:15. *those you have given him.* Again God's initiative in salvation is stressed.
**17:3** *sent.* Again the mission of Jesus is mentioned.
**17:4** *I have brought you glory.* Christ's mission was not self-centered. *the work you gave me.* Jesus emphasized the supreme place of the Father.
**17:5** *glorify me . . . with the glory I had with you.* Jesus asks the Father to return him to his previous position of glory, to exchange humiliation for glorification. This occurred at Christ's resurrection and exaltation to God's right hand. *world.* The universe (see notes on v. 14; 1:9). "World" occurs 18 times in this prayer.
**17:6** *I have revealed you.* See NIV text note and notes on 2:23; 14:13; cf. 1:18. *those whom you gave me.* Again the divine initiative (cf. 6:44).

7Now they know that everything you
have given me comes from you. 8For I
gave them the words you gave me[z]
and they accepted them. They knew
with certainty that I came from you,[a]
and they believed that you sent me.[b]
9I pray for them.[c] I am not praying for
the world, but for those you have giv-
en me,[d] for they are yours. 10All I
have is yours, and all you have is
mine.[e] And glory has come to me
through them. 11I will remain in the
world no longer, but they are still in
the world,[f] and I am coming to you.[g]
Holy Father, protect them by the
power of your name—the name you
gave me—so that they may be one[h]
as we are one.[i] 12While I was with
them, I protected them and kept them
safe by that name you gave me. None
has been lost[j] except the one doomed
to destruction[k] so that Scripture
would be fulfilled.[l]

13"I am coming to you now,[m] but I
say these things while I am still in the
world, so that they may have the full
measure of my joy[n] within them. 14I
have given them your word and the
world has hated them,[o] for they are
not of the world any more than I am
of the world.[p] 15My prayer is not that
you take them out of the world but
that you protect them from the evil
one.[q] 16They are not of the world,
even as I am not of it.[r] 17Sanctify[z]
them by the truth; your word is
truth.[s] 18As you sent me into the
world,[t] I have sent them into the
world.[u] 19For them I sanctify myself,
that they too may be truly sanctified.[v]

## *Jesus Prays for All Believers*

20"My prayer is not for them alone.
I pray also for those who will believe
in me through their message, 21that all
of them may be one,[w] Father, just as
you are in me and I am in you.[x] May
they also be in us so that the world
may believe that you have sent me.[y]
22I have given them the glory that you
gave me,[z] that they may be one as we
are one:[a] 23I in them and you in me.

**17:8** [z]ver 14,26; S Jn 14:24 [a]S Jn 13:3 [b]ver 3, 18,21,23,25; S Jn 3:17 **17:9** [c]Lk 22:32 [d]S ver 2 **17:10** [e]Jn 16:15 **17:11** [f]Jn 13:1 [g]ver 13; Jn 7:33 [h]ver 21-23; Ps 133:1 [i]Jn 10:30 **17:12** [j]S Jn 6:39 [k]Jn 6:70 [l]S Mt 1:22 **17:13** [m]ver 11 [n]S Jn 3:29

**17:14** [o]Jn 15:19 [p]ver 16; Jn 8:23 **17:15** [q]S Mt 5:37 **17:16** [r]ver 14 **17:17** [s]S Jn 15:3; 2Sa 7:28; 1Ki 17:24 **17:18** [t]ver 3,8, 21,23,25; S Jn 3:17 [u]Jn 20:21 **17:19** [v]ver 17 **17:21** [w]Jer 32:39 [x]ver 11; Jn 10:38 [y]ver 3,8,18,23, 25; S Jn 3:17 **17:22** [z]Jn 1:14 [a]S Jn 14:20

[z]17 Greek *hagiazo (set apart for sacred use* or *make holy)*; also in verse 19

**17:7** *everything . . . comes from you.* Only as people see the Father at work in Jesus do they have a proper concept of God. The disciples had at last reached this understanding.
**17:8** Three things about the disciples are mentioned: 1. They accepted the teaching (unlike the Pharisees and others who heard it but did not receive it). 2. They knew with certainty Jesus' divine origin. Acceptance of the revelation led them further into truth. 3. They believed (see note on 1:7; cf. 1:12; 20:31).
**17:9** *not . . . for the world.* The only prayer Jesus could pray for the world was that it cease to be worldly (i.e., opposed to God), and this he did pray (vv. 21,23).
**17:11** *Holy Father.* A form of address found only here in the NT (but cf. 1Pe 1:15–16; Rev 4:8; 6:10). The name suggests both remoteness and nearness; God is both awe-inspiring and loving. *that they may be one.* The latter part of the prayer strongly emphasizes unity. Here the unity is already given, not something to be achieved. The meaning is "that they continually be one" rather than "that they become one." The unity is to be like that between the Father and the Son. It is much more than unity of organization, but the church's present divisions are the result of the failures of Christians.
**17:12** *I protected them.* Christ's power is adequate for every need. *the one doomed to destruction.* Lit. "the son of destruction" (see 2Th 2:3), i.e., one belonging to the sphere of damnation and destined for destruction (but predestination is not here in view).
**17:13** *my joy.* See note on 15:11.
**17:14** *the world.* The world that is hostile to God and God's people (see notes on v. 5; 1:9). *not of the world.* They do not have the mind-set of the world, i.e., hostility to God, for they have been "born of the Spirit" (3:8) and are "children of God" (1:12).
**17:15** *not that you take them out of the world.* The world is where Jesus' disciples are to do their work; Jesus does not wish them to be taken from it until that work is done (see v. 18). *the evil one.* Especially active in the world (1Jn 5:19), making God's protection indispensable.
**17:17** *Sanctify.* See NIV text note. *the truth; your word.* Sanctification and revelation (as recorded in God's word) go together. For the connection of Christ's teaching with truth cf. 8:31–32.
**17:18** *As you sent me . . . I have sent them.* Jesus' mission is one of the dominant themes of this Gospel and is given as the pattern for his followers. *into the world.* We may long for heaven, but it is on earth that our work is done.
**17:19** *I sanctify myself.* This statement appears to be unparalleled. In the Septuagint (the Greek translation of the OT) the verb is used of consecrating priests (Ex 28:41) and sacrifices (Ex 28:38; Nu 18:9). Jesus solemnly "sets himself apart to do God's will," which at this point meant his death. *that they too may be . . . sanctified.* Jesus died on the cross not only to save us but also to consecrate us to God's service (see NIV text note on v. 17).
**17:20** *those who will believe in me.* Jesus had just spoken of the mission and the sanctification of his followers (vv. 18–19). He was confident that they would spread the gospel, and he prayed for those who would believe as a result. All future believers are included in this prayer.
**17:21** *that all of them may be one.* See note on v. 11. *Father.* See note on v. 1. *that the world may believe.* The unity of believers should have an effect on outsiders, to convince them of the mission of Christ. Jesus' prayer is a rebuke of the groundless and often bitter divisions among believers.
**17:22** *the glory.* See note on v. 1. Believers are to be characterized by humility and service, just as Christ was, and it is on them that God's glory rests. *that they may be one as we are one.* Again the Lord emphasized the importance of unity among his followers, and again the standard is the unity of the Father and the Son.
**17:23** *I in them and you in me.* There are two indwellings: that of the Son in believers, and that of the Father in the Son. It is because the latter is a reality that the former can take place. *complete unity.* Again the emphasis on unity has an

May they be brought to complete unity to let the world know that you sent
me[b] and have loved them[c] even as
you have loved me.
24"Father, I want those you have
given me[d] to be with me where I
am,[e] and to see my glory,[f] the glory
you have given me because you loved
me before the creation of the world.[g]
25"Righteous Father, though the
world does not know you,[h] I know
you, and they know that you have
sent me.[i] 26I have made you known
to them,[j] and will continue to make
you known in order that the love you
have for me may be in them[k] and that
I myself may be in them."

## Jesus Arrested

*18:3–11pp — Mt 26:47–56; Mk 14:43–50; Lk 22:47–53*

18 When he had finished praying,
Jesus left with his disciples and
crossed the Kidron Valley.[l] On the other
side there was an olive grove,[m] and he and
his disciples went into it.[n]
2Now Judas, who betrayed him, knew
the place, because Jesus had often met
there with his disciples.[o] 3So Judas came
to the grove, guiding[p] a detachment of soldiers and some officials from the chief
priests and Pharisees.[q] They were carrying
torches, lanterns and weapons.
4Jesus, knowing all that was going to
happen to him,[r] went out and asked
them, "Who is it you want?"[s]
5"Jesus of Nazareth,"[t] they replied.
"I am he," Jesus said. (And Judas the
traitor was standing there with them.)
6When Jesus said, "I am he," they drew
back and fell to the ground.
7Again he asked them, "Who is it you
want?"[u]
And they said, "Jesus of Nazareth."
8"I told you that I am he," Jesus answered. "If you are looking for me, then
let these men go." 9This happened so that
the words he had spoken would be fulfilled: "I have not lost one of those you
gave me."[a] [v]
10Then Simon Peter, who had a sword,
drew it and struck the high priest's servant, cutting off his right ear. (The servant's name was Malchus.)
11Jesus commanded Peter, "Put your
sword away! Shall I not drink the cup[w] the
Father has given me?"

## Jesus Taken to Annas

*18:12,13pp — Mt 26:57*

12Then the detachment of soldiers with
its commander and the Jewish officials[x]
arrested Jesus. They bound him 13and
brought him first to Annas, who was the
father-in-law of Caiaphas,[y] the high priest
that year. 14Caiaphas was the one who had

**17:23** [b]ver 3,8, 18,21,25; S Jn 3:17 [c]Jn 16:27 **17:24** [d]S ver 2 [e]S Jn 12:26 [f]Jn 1:14 [g]ver 5; S Mt 25:34; S Jn 1:2 **17:25** [h]Jn 15:21; 16:3 [i]ver 3,8,18, 21,23; S Jn 3:17; 16:27 **17:26** [j]ver 6 [k]Jn 15:9 **18:1** [l]2Sa 15:23 [m]ver 26; S Mt 21:1 [n]Mt 26:36 **18:2** [o]Lk 21:37; 22:39 **18:3** [p]Ac 1:16 [q]ver 12

**18:4** [r]Jn 6:64; 13:1,11 [s]ver 7 **18:5** [t]S Mk 1:24 **18:7** [u]ver 4 **18:9** [v]S Jn 6:39 **18:11** [w]S Mt 20:22 **18:12** [x]ver 3 **18:13** [y]ver 24; S Mt 26:3

[a]9 John 6:39

evangelistic aim. This time it is connected not only with the mission of Jesus but also with God's love for people and for Christ.

**17:24** *Father.* See note on v. 1. *I want.* Means "I will that." Jesus said, "I will"—his last will and testament for his followers. Where he himself was concerned, he prayed, "not what I will, but what you will" (Mk 14:36). *to be with me.* The Christian's greatest blessing. *my glory.* Perhaps used here to refer to Jesus' eternal splendor (see 1Jn 3:2). Or Jesus' prayer may have been that in the life to come they might fully appreciate the glory of his lowly service (cf. Eph 2:7).

**17:25** *Righteous Father.* A form of address found only here in the NT (cf. "Holy Father," v. 11). *they know.* They did not know God directly and personally, but they knew God had sent Christ. To recognize God in Christ's mission is a great advance over anything the world can know.

**18:1** *crossed the Kidron Valley.* East of Jerusalem and dry except during the rainy season.

**18:3** *Judas.* See note on 6:71. *officials from the chief priests and Pharisees.* Equivalent to the temple guard sent by the Sanhedrin. *torches.* Resinous pieces of wood fastened together. *lanterns.* Terra-cotta holders into which household lamps could be inserted.

**18:4** *knowing all that was going to happen to him.* Jesus was not taken by surprise.

**18:5** *I am.* See 6:35; 8:58 and notes. *with them.* John does not let us forget where Judas belonged.

**18:6** *fell to the ground.* They came to arrest a meek peasant and instead were met in the dim light by a majestic person.

**18:8** *I am.* The threefold repetition (vv. 5,6,8) emphasizes the solemn words. *let these men go.* Jesus cared for the disciples even as he was going to his death. Twice he had made the arresting party say plainly that he was the one they wanted (vv. 4–5,7).

**18:9** *would be fulfilled.* Words normally used in quoting Scripture, and Jesus' words are on the same level. See 6:39; 17:12.

**18:10** *Simon Peter.* It is to John that we owe the information that the man with the sword (the Greek for this word refers to a short sword) was Peter, and that the man he wounded was named Malchus.

**18:11** *the cup.* Often points to suffering (Ps 75:8; Eze 23:31–34) and the wrath of God (Isa 51:17,22; Jer 25:15; Rev 14:10; 16:19). *the Father has given me.* The Synoptic Gospels also speak of the cup at the time of Jesus' prayer at Gethsemane (Mt 26:39; Mk 14:36; Lk 22:42), and John says it came from the Father. God was in control.

**18:12** *bound him.* The reason for the bonds is not clear. Perhaps their use was standard procedure, much like the modern use of handcuffs.

**18:13** *Annas.* Had been deposed from the high priesthood by the Romans in A.D. 15 but was probably still regarded by many as the true high priest. In Jewish law a man could not be sentenced on the day his trial was held. The two examinations—this one (mentioned only by John) and that before Caiaphas—may have been conducted to give some form of legitimacy to what was done. *high priest that year.* See note on 11:49.

**18:14** *Caiaphas . . . had advised the Jews.* A reference to

advised the Jews that it would be good if
one man died for the people.[z]

### *Peter's First Denial*

*18:16–18pp — Mt 26:69,70; Mk 14:66–68; Lk 22:55–57*

15 Simon Peter and another disciple were
following Jesus. Because this disciple was
known to the high priest,[a] he went with
Jesus into the high priest's courtyard,[b]
16 but Peter had to wait outside at the door.
The other disciple, who was known to the
high priest, came back, spoke to the girl on
duty there and brought Peter in.
17 "You are not one of his disciples, are
you?" the girl at the door asked Peter.
He replied, "I am not."[c]
18 It was cold, and the servants and officials stood around a fire[d] they had made to
keep warm. Peter also was standing with
them, warming himself.[e]

### *The High Priest Questions Jesus*

*18:19–24pp — Mt 26:59–68; Mk 14:55–65; Lk 22:63–71*

19 Meanwhile, the high priest questioned
Jesus about his disciples and his teaching.
20 "I have spoken openly to the world,"
Jesus replied. "I always taught in synagogues[f] or at the temple,[g] where all the
Jews come together. I said nothing in secret.[h] 21 Why question me? Ask those who
heard me. Surely they know what I said."

**18:14** [z]Jn 11:49-51 **18:15** [a]S Mt 26:3 [b]Mt 26:58; Mk 14:54; Lk 22:54 **18:17** [c]ver 25 **18:18** [d]Jn 21:9 [e]Mk 14:54,67 **18:20** [f]S Mt 4:23 [g]Mt 26:55 [h]Jn 7:26

**18:22** [i]ver 3 [j]Mt 16:21; Jn 19:3 **18:23** [k]Mt 5:39; Ac 23:2-5 **18:24** [l]ver 13; S Mt 26:3 **18:25** [m]ver 18 [n]ver 17 **18:26** [o]ver 10 [p]ver 1 **18:27** [q]Jn 13:38 **18:28** [r]S Mt 27:2

22 When Jesus said this, one of the officials[i] nearby struck him in the face.[j] "Is
this the way you answer the high priest?"
he demanded.
23 "If I said something wrong," Jesus replied, "testify as to what is wrong. But if I
spoke the truth, why did you strike me?"[k]
24 Then Annas sent him, still bound, to
Caiaphas[l] the high priest.[b]

### *Peter's Second and Third Denials*

*18:25–27pp — Mt 26:71–75; Mk 14:69–72; Lk 22:58–62*

25 As Simon Peter stood warming himself,[m] he was asked, "You are not one of
his disciples, are you?"
He denied it, saying, "I am not."[n]
26 One of the high priest's servants, a
relative of the man whose ear Peter had
cut off,[o] challenged him, "Didn't I see you
with him in the olive grove?"[p] 27 Again Peter denied it, and at that moment a rooster
began to crow.[q]

### *Jesus Before Pilate*

*18:29–40pp — Mt 27:11–18,20–23; Mk 15:2–15; Lk 23:2,3,18–25*

28 Then the Jews led Jesus from Caiaphas
to the palace of the Roman governor.[r] By
now it was early morning, and to avoid

[b]24 Or *(Now Annas had sent him, still bound, to Caiaphas the high priest.)*

---

11:49–50. For John it was this unconscious prophecy that mattered most about Caiaphas. John may also have been hinting that a fair trial could not be expected from a man who had already said that putting Jesus to death was expedient.
**18:15** *another disciple.* Perhaps John himself. *known to the high priest.* Refers to more than casual acquaintance; he had entrée into the high priest's house and could bring Peter in.
**18:17** *the girl at the door.* All four Gospels tell us that Peter's first challenge came from a slave girl, the most unimportant person imaginable. Her question expected the answer "No." Peter took the easy way out. The other Gospels seem to indicate that the other denials followed immediately, but it is likely that there were intervals during which other things happened (see Lk 22:58–59).
**18:18** *Peter also was standing with them.* On a cold night he would have been conspicuous if he had stayed away from the fire.
**18:19** *questioned.* Not legal, since witnesses were supposed to be brought in first to establish guilt. The accused was not required to prove his innocence. Perhaps Annas regarded this as a preliminary inquiry, not a trial.
**18:20** *I have spoken openly.* It should not have been difficult to find witnesses (v. 21). *nothing in secret.* Not a denial that he taught the disciples privately, but a denial that he had secretly taught them subversive teaching different from his public message.
**18:22** *struck.* Another illegality. The word apparently means a blow with the open hand—a slap.
**18:23** *testify.* A legal term, indicating an invitation to act in proper legal form. John stresses the importance of testimony throughout his Gospel (see note on 1:7).
**18:25** *he was asked.* Lit. "they asked him." Some find a difficulty in that Mt 26:71 says another girl asked this question, whereas Mk 14:69 says it was the same girl, and Lk 22:58 that it was a man. But with a group of servants talking around a fire, several would doubtless take up and repeat such a question, which could be the meaning of John's "they." As on the first occasion (v. 17) the question anticipated the answer "No." The servants probably did not really expect to find a follower of Jesus in the high priest's courtyard, but the question seemed worth asking.
**18:26** *a relative.* Another piece of information we owe to John. A relative would have a deeper interest in the swordsman than other people had. But the light in the garden would have been dim, as in the courtyard (a charcoal fire glows, but does not have flames). *Didn't I see you . . . ?* Expected the answer "Yes."
**18:27** *a rooster began to crow.* The fulfillment of the prophecy in 13:38.
**18:28** *the Roman governor.* John says little about the Jewish phase of Jesus' trial but much about the Roman trial (see note on Mk 14:53–15:15). It is possible that John was in the Praetorium, the governor's official residence, for this trial. *early morning.* The chief priests evidently held a second session of the Sanhedrin after daybreak to give some appearance of legality to what they did (Mk 15:1). This occasion would have been immediately after that, perhaps between 6:00 A.M. and 7:00 A.M. *ceremonial uncleanness.* A result of entering a Gentile residence. *to eat the Passover.* Does not mean that the time of the Passover meal had not yet come, for this would contradict the Synoptic Gospels, which have Jesus eating the Passover meal the night before. The term "Passover" was used to refer to the whole festival of Passover and Unleavened Bread, which lasted seven days and included a number of meals.

ceremonial uncleanness the Jews did not
enter the palace;[s] they wanted to be able
to eat the Passover.[t] 29So Pilate came out
to them and asked, "What charges are you
bringing against this man?"
30"If he were not a criminal," they replied, "we would not have handed him
over to you."
31Pilate said, "Take him yourselves and
judge him by your own law."
"But we have no right to execute anyone," the Jews objected. 32This happened
so that the words Jesus had spoken indicating the kind of death he was going to die[u]
would be fulfilled.
33Pilate then went back inside the palace,[v] summoned Jesus and asked him,
"Are you the king of the Jews?"[w]
34"Is that your own idea," Jesus asked,
"or did others talk to you about me?"
35"Am I a Jew?" Pilate replied. "It was
your people and your chief priests who
handed you over to me. What is it you
have done?"
36Jesus said, "My kingdom[x] is not of
this world. If it were, my servants would
fight to prevent my arrest by the Jews.[y]
But now my kingdom is from another
place."[z]
37"You are a king, then!" said Pilate.
Jesus answered, "You are right in saying
I am a king. In fact, for this reason I was
born, and for this I came into the world, to
testify to the truth.[a] Everyone on the side
of truth listens to me."[b]
38"What is truth?" Pilate asked. With
this he went out again to the Jews and
said, "I find no basis for a charge against
him.[c] 39But it is your custom for me to
release to you one prisoner at the time of
the Passover. Do you want me to release
'the king of the Jews'?"
40They shouted back, "No, not him!
Give us Barabbas!" Now Barabbas had tak-
en part in a rebellion.[d]

## *Jesus Sentenced to be Crucified*

*19:1–16pp — Mt 27:27–31; Mk 15:16–20*

19 Then Pilate took Jesus and had him
flogged.[e] 2The soldiers twisted together a crown of thorns and put it on his
head. They clothed him in a purple robe
3and went up to him again and again, saying, "Hail, king of the Jews!"[f] And they
struck him in the face.[g]
4Once more Pilate came out and said to
the Jews, "Look, I am bringing him out[h]
to you to let you know that I find no basis
for a charge against him."[i] 5When Jesus
came out wearing the crown of thorns and
the purple robe,[j] Pilate said to them,
"Here is the man!"
6As soon as the chief priests and their
officials saw him, they shouted, "Crucify!
Crucify!"
But Pilate answered, "You take him and
crucify him.[k] As for me, I find no basis for
a charge against him."[l]
7The Jews insisted, "We have a law, and
according to that law he must die,[m] be-

**18:28** [s]ver 33; Jn 19:9 [t]Jn 11:55 **18:32** [u]Mt 20:19; 26:2; Jn 3:14; 8:28; 12:32,33 **18:33** [v]ver 28, 29; Jn 19:9 [w]Lk 23:3; S Mt 2:2 **18:36** [x]S Mt 3:2 [y]Mt 26:53 [z]Lk 17:21; Jn 6:15 **18:37** [a]Jn 3:32 [b]Jn 8:47; 1Jn 4:6 **18:38** [c]S Lk 23:4 **18:40** [d]Ac 3:14 **19:1** [e]Dt 25:3; Isa 50:6; 53:5; Mt 27:26 **19:3** [f]Mt 27:29 [g]Jn 18:22 **19:4** [h]Jn 18:38 [i]ver 6; S Lk 23:4 **19:5** [j]ver 2 **19:6** [k]Ac 3:13 [l]ver 4; S Lk 23:4 **19:7** [m]Lev 24:16

**18:29** *Pilate.* The Roman governor (see note on Mk 15:1). He showed himself tolerant of Jewish ways. *What charges . . . ?* A normal question at the beginning of a trial, but it was difficult to answer, because the Jews had no charge that would stand up in a Roman court of law.
**18:31** *Take him yourselves.* In other words, no Roman charge, no Roman trial. *no right to execute anyone.* They were looking for an execution, not a fair trial. The restriction was important, for otherwise Rome's supporters could be quietly removed by local legal executions. Sometimes the Romans seem to have condoned local executions (e.g., of Stephen, Ac 7), but normally they retained the right to inflict the death penalty.
**18:32** *the kind of death he was going to die.* Cf. 12:32–33 and "must" in 12:34. Jewish execution was by stoning, but Jesus' death was to be by crucifixion, whereby he would bear the curse (Dt 21:22–23). The Romans, not the Jews, had to put Jesus to death. God was overruling in the whole process.
**18:33** *Are you the king of the Jews?* Pilate's first words to Jesus, identical in all four Gospels. One glance was enough to show him that a dangerous rebel existed only in the imaginations of Jesus' enemies.
**18:34** *Is that your own idea . . . ?* If so, Pilate's question (v. 33) had meant, "Are you a rebel?" If the question had originated with the Jews, it meant, "Are you the Messianic King?"
**18:36** *My kingdom.* Jesus agrees that he has a kingdom, but asserts that it is not the kind of kingdom that has soldiers to fight for it. It was not built, nor is it maintained, by military might.
**18:37** *to testify to the truth.* Two of this Gospel's important ideas (see 1:7 and note; 1:14 and note; 14:6).
**18:38** *What is truth?* Pilate may have been jesting, and meant, "What does truth matter?" Or he may have been serious, and meant, "It is not easy to find truth. What is it?" Either way, it was clear to him that Jesus was no rebel. *no basis for a charge against him.* Teaching the truth was not a criminal offense.
**18:39** *it is your custom.* Prisoners are known to have been released on special occasions in other places. *the king of the Jews.* John keeps his emphasis on the note of royalty. Pilate may have hoped that the use of the title would influence the people toward the way he wanted them to decide.
**18:40** *Barabbas.* A rebel and a murderer (Lk 23:19). The name is Aramaic and means "son of Abba," i.e., "son of the father"; in place of this man, the "Son of the Father" died.
**19:1** Pilate hoped a flogging would satisfy the Jews and enable him to release Jesus (see note on Mk 15:15).
**19:2** *thorns.* A general term relating to any thorny plant. *purple.* A color used by royalty.
**19:6** *You . . . crucify him.* The petulant utterance of an exasperated man, for the Jews could not carry out this form of execution. *I find no basis.* For the third time Pilate proclaimed Jesus' innocence (see 18:38; 19:4). Luke also records this threefold proclamation (Lk 23:4,14,22).
**19:7** *he must die.* Apparently referring to the penalty for

cause he claimed to be the Son of God."[n]

8When Pilate heard this, he was even more afraid, 9and he went back inside the palace.[o] "Where do you come from?" he asked Jesus, but Jesus gave him no answer.[p] 10"Do you refuse to speak to me?" Pilate said. "Don't you realize I have power either to free you or to crucify you?"

11Jesus answered, "You would have no power over me if it were not given to you from above.[q] Therefore the one who handed me over to you[r] is guilty of a greater sin."

12From then on, Pilate tried to set Jesus free, but the Jews kept shouting, "If you let this man go, you are no friend of Caesar. Anyone who claims to be a king[s] opposes Caesar."

13When Pilate heard this, he brought Jesus out and sat down on the judge's seat[t] at a place known as the Stone Pavement (which in Aramaic[u] is Gabbatha). 14It was the day of Preparation[v] of Passover Week, about the sixth hour.[w]

"Here is your king,"[x] Pilate said to the Jews.

15But they shouted, "Take him away! Take him away! Crucify him!"

"Shall I crucify your king?" Pilate asked.

"We have no king but Caesar," the chief priests answered.

16Finally Pilate handed him over to them to be crucified.[y]

## The Crucifixion

*19:17–24pp — Mt 27:33–44; Mk 15:22–32; Lk 23:33–43*

So the soldiers took charge of Jesus. 17Carrying his own cross,[z] he went out to the place of the Skull[a] (which in Aramaic[b] is called Golgotha). 18Here they crucified him, and with him two others[c]—one on each side and Jesus in the middle.

19Pilate had a notice prepared and fastened to the cross. It read: JESUS OF NAZARETH,[d] THE KING OF THE JEWS.[e] 20Many of the Jews read this sign, for the place where Jesus was crucified was near the city,[f] and the sign was written in Aramaic, Latin and Greek. 21The chief priests of the Jews protested to Pilate, "Do not write 'The King of the Jews,' but that this man claimed to be king of the Jews."[g]

22Pilate answered, "What I have written, I have written."

23When the soldiers crucified Jesus, they took his clothes, dividing them into four shares, one for each of them, with the un-

**19:7** [n]Mt 26:63-66; Jn 5:18; 10:33
**19:9** [o]Jn 18:33 [p]S Mk 14:61
**19:11** [q]S Ro 13:1 [r]Jn 18:28-30; Ac 3:13
**19:12** [s]Lk 23:2
**19:13** [t]Mt 27:19 [u]S Jn 5:2
**19:14** [v]Mt 27:62 [w]Mk 15:25 [x]ver 19,21
**19:16** [y]Mt 27:26; Mk 15:15; Lk 23:25
**19:17** [z]Ge 22:6; Lk 14:27; 23:26 [a]Lk 23:33 [b]S Jn 5:2
**19:18** [c]Lk 23:32
**19:19** [d]S Mk 1:24 [e]ver 14,21
**19:20** [f]Heb 13:12
**19:21** [g]ver 14

---

blasphemy (Lev 24:16).

**19:8** *even more afraid.* Pilate was evidently superstitious, and this charge frightened him.

**19:9** *Jesus gave him no answer.* The reason is not clear, but Jesus had answered other questions readily. Perhaps Pilate would not have understood the answer or would not have believed it.

**19:10** *I have power.* Pilate was incredulous and very conscious of his authority. His second question indicates his personal responsibility for crucifying Jesus.

**19:11** Jesus' last words to Pilate. *from above.* All earthly authority comes ultimately from God. *a greater sin.* That of Caiaphas (not Judas, who was only a means). But "greater" implies that there was a lesser sin, so Pilate's sin was also real.

**19:12** *no friend of Caesar.* Some people had official status as "Friends of Caesar," but the term seems to be used here in the general sense. There was an implied threat that if he released Jesus, Pilate would be accused before Caesar. His record was such that he could not face such a prospect without concern.

**19:13** *the Stone Pavement.* Not a translation of *Gabbatha,* which seems to mean "the hill of the house," but a different name for the same place.

**19:14** *day of Preparation.* Normally Friday was the day people prepared for the Sabbath. Here the meaning is Friday of Passover week. *about the sixth hour.* About noon. Mk 15:25 says that Jesus was crucified at "the third hour." It is possible that Mark's Gospel contains a copyist's error, for the Greek numerals for three and six could be confused. Or it may be that John was using Roman time, in which case the appearance before Pilate would have been at 6:00 A.M. and the crucifixion at 9:00 A.M. (the third hour according to Jewish reckoning; see Mk 15:33). For other time references see Mt 27:45–46; Mk 15: 33–34; Lk 23:44. *Here is your king.* John does not let us forget the sovereignty of Jesus. Pilate did not mean the expression seriously, but John did. *the Jews.* See note on 1:19.

**19:15** *We have no king but Caesar.* More irony. They rejected any suggestion that they were rebels against Rome, but expressed the truth of their spiritual condition.

**19:17** *Carrying his own cross.* A cross might be shaped like a *T,* an *X,* a *Y,* or an *I,* as well as like the traditional form. A condemned man would normally carry a beam of it to the place of execution. Somewhere along the way Simon of Cyrene took Jesus' cross (Mk 15:21), probably because Jesus was weakened by the flogging. *Golgotha.* Aramaic for "the skull." The name of the site is given in both Greek and Aramaic ("Calvary" is from the Latin with the same meaning). See note on Mk 15:22.

**19:18** *they crucified him.* See note on Mk 15:24. As with the scourging, John describes this horror with one Greek word. None of the Gospel writers dwells on the physical sufferings of Jesus. *one on each side.* Perhaps meant as a final insult, but it brings out the important truth that in his death Jesus was identified with sinners.

**19:19** *a notice.* A placard stating the crime for which a man was executed was often fastened to his cross. *THE KING OF THE JEWS.* Again the royalty theme.

**19:20** *Aramaic.* One of the languages of the Jewish people at that time (along with Hebrew). *Latin.* The official language of Rome. *Greek.* The common language of communication throughout the empire. The threefold inscription may account for the slight differences in wording in the four Gospels.

**19:22** Pilate must have a sufficient reason for the execution, and he was not above mocking the Jews, but for John his insistence may also have served to underscore that Jesus' kingship is final and unalterable.

**19:23** *undergarment.* A type of shirt, reaching from the

dergarment remaining. This garment was
seamless, woven in one piece from top to
bottom.
24“Let's not tear it,” they said to one
another. “Let's decide by lot who will get
it.”
This happened that the scripture might
be fulfilled[h] which said,

“They divided my garments among
them
and cast lots for my clothing.”[c] [i]

So this is what the soldiers did.
25Near the cross[j] of Jesus stood his
mother,[k] his mother's sister, Mary the
wife of Clopas, and Mary Magdalene.[l]
26When Jesus saw his mother[m] there, and
the disciple whom he loved[n] standing
nearby, he said to his mother, “Dear
woman, here is your son,” 27and to the
disciple, “Here is your mother.” From that
time on, this disciple took her into his
home.

### *The Death of Jesus*

*19:29,30pp — Mt 27:48,50; Mk 15:36,37; Lk 23:36*

28Later, knowing that all was now completed,[o] and so that the Scripture would
be fulfilled,[p] Jesus said, “I am thirsty.” 29A
jar of wine vinegar[q] was there, so they
soaked a sponge in it, put the sponge on a
stalk of the hyssop plant, and lifted it to
Jesus' lips. 30When he had received the
drink, Jesus said, “It is finished.”[r] With
that, he bowed his head and gave up his
spirit.
31Now it was the day of Preparation,[s]
and the next day was to be a special Sabbath. Because the Jews did not want the
bodies left on the crosses[t] during the Sabbath, they asked Pilate to have the legs
broken and the bodies taken down. 32The
soldiers therefore came and broke the legs
of the first man who had been crucified
with Jesus, and then those of the other.[u]
33But when they came to Jesus and found
that he was already dead, they did not
break his legs. 34Instead, one of the soldiers
pierced[v] Jesus' side with a spear, bringing
a sudden flow of blood and water.[w] 35The
man who saw it[x] has given testimony, and
his testimony is true.[y] He knows that he
tells the truth, and he testifies so that you
also may believe. 36These things happened
so that the scripture would be fulfilled:[z]
“Not one of his bones will be broken,”[d] [a]
37and, as another scripture says, “They will
look on the one they have pierced.”[e] [b]

### *The Burial of Jesus*

*19:38–42pp — Mt 27:57–61; Mk 15:42–47; Lk 23:50–56*

38Later, Joseph of Arimathea asked Pilate for the body of Jesus. Now Joseph was
a disciple of Jesus, but secretly because he
feared the Jews.[c] With Pilate's permission,
he came and took the body away. 39He
was accompanied by Nicodemus,[d] the

**19:24** [h]ver 28, 36,37; S Mt 1:22 [i]Ps 22:18 **19:25** [j]Mt 27:55, 56 [k]S Mt 12:46 [l]Lk 8:2; Jn 20:1, 18 **19:26** [m]S Mt 12:46 [n]S Jn 13:23 **19:28** [o]S ver 30; Jn 13:1 [p]ver 24, 36,37; S Mt 1:22 **19:29** [q]Ps 69:21 **19:30** [r]Lk 12:50; Jn 4:34; 17:4 **19:31** [s]ver 14,42 [t]Dt 21:23; Jos 8:29; 10:26, 27 **19:32** [u]ver 18 **19:34** [v]Zec 12:10; Rev 1:7 [w]1Jn 5:6, 8 **19:35** [x]S Lk 24:48 [y]Jn 15:27; 21:24 **19:36** [z]ver 24,28, 37; S Mt 1:22 [a]Ex 12:46; Nu 9:12; Ps 34:20 **19:37** [b]Zec 12:10; Rev 1:7 **19:38** [c]S Jn 7:13 **19:39** [d]Jn 3:1; 7:50

[c]*24* Psalm 22:18 [d]*36* Exodus 12:46; Num. 9:12; Psalm 34:20 [e]*37* Zech. 12:10

neck to the knees or ankles. *seamless.* Therefore too valuable to be cut up.

**19:24** See introduction to Ps 22 and notes on Ps 22:17, 20–21.

**19:25** *Clopas.* Mentioned only here in the NT. *Mary Magdalene.* Appears in the crucifixion and resurrection story in all four Gospels, but apart from that we read of her only in Lk 8:2–3.

**19:26** *disciple whom he loved.* John (see note on 13:23).

**19:27** *took her into his home.* And so took responsibility for her. It may be that Jesus' brothers still did not believe in him (see 7:5).

**19:28** *I am thirsty.* May refer to Ps 69:21 (cf. Ps 22:15).

**19:29** *wine vinegar.* Equivalent to cheap wine, the drink of ordinary people. *a sponge.* A useful way of giving drink to one on a cross, and may indicate forethought and compassion on someone's part. *hyssop.* The name given to a number of plants. See also note on Ex 12:22.

**19:30** *It is finished.* Apparently the loud cry of Mt 27:50; Mk 15:37. Jesus died as a victor and had completed what he came to do. *gave up his spirit.* An unusual way of describing death, perhaps suggesting an act of will.

**19:31** *Preparation.* See note on v. 14. *a special Sabbath.* The Sabbath that fell at Passover time. The Passover meal had been eaten on Thursday evening, the day of Preparation was Friday, and the Sabbath came on Saturday. *the Jews.* See note on 1:19. *to have the legs broken.* To hasten death, because the victim then could not put any weight on his legs and breathing would be difficult.

**19:34** *pierced Jesus' side.* Probably to make doubly sure that Jesus was dead, but perhaps simply an act of brutality (see v. 37; Isa 53:5; Zec 12:10; cf. Ps 22:16). *blood and water.* The result of the spear piercing the pericardium (the sac that surrounds the heart) and the heart itself.

**19:35** *The man who saw it.* Either John himself or someone he regarded as reliable. Obviously he considered the incident important, and comments that it was well attested. *testifies . . . believe.* See note on 1:7.

**19:36–37** *scripture.* Again John observes God's overruling in the fulfillment of Scripture. It was extraordinary that Jesus was the only one of the three whose legs were not broken and that he suffered an unusual spear thrust that did not break a bone.

**19:38** *Joseph.* A rich disciple (Mt 27:57), and a member of the Sanhedrin who had not agreed to Jesus' condemnation (Lk 23:51). *Arimathea.* See note on Mt 27:57. *secretly.* It would have been hard for a member of the Sanhedrin to support Jesus' cause openly. Jesus' closest followers all ran away (Mk 14:50), and it was left to Joseph and Nicodemus to provide for his burial. *With Pilate's permission.* Otherwise people could take away their crucified friends before they died and revive them.

**19:39** *Nicodemus.* John alone tells us that he joined Joseph in the burial. *seventy-five pounds.* A very large amount, such as was used in royal burials (cf. 2Ch 16:14).

man who earlier had visited Jesus at night.
Nicodemus brought a mixture of myrrh
and aloes, about seventy-five pounds.[f]
40Taking Jesus' body, the two of them
wrapped it, with the spices, in strips of
linen.[e] This was in accordance with
Jewish burial customs.[f] 41At the place
where Jesus was crucified, there was a garden, and in the garden a new tomb, in
which no one had ever been laid. 42Be-
cause it was the Jewish day of Preparation[g] and since the tomb was nearby,[h]
they laid Jesus there.

## *The Empty Tomb*

*20:1–8pp — Mt 28:1–8; Mk 16:1–8; Lk 24:1–10*

20 Early on the first day of the week,
while it was still dark, Mary Magdalene[i] went to the tomb and saw that
the stone had been removed from the entrance.[j] 2So she came running to Simon
Peter and the other disciple, the one Jesus
loved,[k] and said, "They have taken the
Lord out of the tomb, and we don't know
where they have put him!"[l]
3So Peter and the other disciple started
for the tomb.[m] 4Both were running, but
the other disciple outran Peter and reached
the tomb first. 5He bent over and looked
in[n] at the strips of linen[o] lying there but
did not go in. 6Then Simon Peter, who was
behind him, arrived and went into the
tomb. He saw the strips of linen lying
there, 7as well as the burial cloth that had
been around Jesus' head.[p] The cloth was
folded up by itself, separate from the linen.
8Finally the other disciple, who had
reached the tomb first,[q] also went inside.
He saw and believed. 9(They still did not
understand from Scripture[r] that Jesus had
to rise from the dead.)[s]

## *Jesus Appears to Mary Magdalene*

10Then the disciples went back to their
homes, 11but Mary stood outside the tomb
crying. As she wept, she bent over to look
into the tomb[t] 12and saw two angels in
white,[u] seated where Jesus' body had
been, one at the head and the other at the
foot.
13They asked her, "Woman, why are
you crying?"[v]
"They have taken my Lord away," she
said, "and I don't know where they have
put him."[w] 14At this, she turned around
and saw Jesus standing there,[x] but she did
not realize that it was Jesus.[y]
15"Woman," he said, "why are you crying?[z] Who is it you are looking for?"
Thinking he was the gardener, she said,
"Sir, if you have carried him away, tell me
where you have put him, and I will get
him."
16Jesus said to her, "Mary."
She turned toward him and cried out in
Aramaic,[a] "Rabboni!"[b] (which means
Teacher).
17Jesus said, "Do not hold on to me, for
I have not yet returned to the Father. Go

**19:40** [e]Lk 24:12; Jn 11:44; 20:5,7 [f]Mt 26:12
**19:42** [g]ver 14,31 [h]ver 20,41
**20:1** [i]ver 18; Lk 8:2; Jn 19:25 [j]Mt 27:60,66
**20:2** [k]S Jn 13:23 [l]ver 13
**20:3** [m]Lk 24:12
**20:5** [n]ver 11 [o]S Jn 19:40
**20:7** [p]Jn 11:44
**20:8** [q]ver 4
**20:9** [r]Mt 22:29; Jn 2:22 [s]Lk 24:26,46; Ac 2:24
**20:11** [t]ver 5
**20:12** [u]Mt 28:2,3; Mk 16:5; Lk 24:4; Ac 1:10; S 5:19; 10:30
**20:13** [v]ver 15 [w]ver 2
**20:14** [x]Mk 16:9 [y]Lk 24:16; Jn 21:4
**20:15** [z]ver 13
**20:16** [a]S Jn 5:2 [b]S Mt 23:7

[f]39 Greek *a hundred litrai* (about 34 kilograms)

**19:40** *strips of linen.* Thin strips like bandages. There was also a shroud, a large sheet (Mt 27:59; Mk 15:46; Lk 23:53).
**19:41** *a new tomb.* Joseph's own tomb (Mt 27:60).
**19:42** *Preparation.* See note on v. 14. *nearby.* Haste was necessary, since it was near sunset, when the Sabbath would start and no work could be done.
**20:1** *while it was still dark.* Mark says it was "just after sunrise" (Mk 16:2). Perhaps the women came in groups, with Mary Magdalene coming very early. Or John may refer to the time of leaving home, Mark to that of arrival at the tomb. *Mary Magdalene.* See note on 19:25; cf. Mk 16:9.
**20:2** *to Simon Peter.* Despite his denials, Peter was still the leading figure among the disciples. *the one Jesus loved.* John (see note on 13:23). *we.* Indicates that there were others with Mary (see Mt 28:1; Mk 16:1; Lk 24:10), though John does not identify them. *have put him.* Mary had no thought of resurrection.
**20:7** *folded up.* An orderly arrangement, not in disarray, as would have resulted from a grave robbery.
**20:8** *He saw and believed.* Cf. v. 29. John did not say what he believed, but it must have been that Jesus was resurrected.
**20:9** *Scripture.* First they came to know of the resurrection through what they saw in the tomb; only later did they see it in Scripture. It is obvious they did not make up a story of resurrection to fit a preconceived understanding of Scriptural prophecy. *had to rise.* It was in Scripture and thus the will of God.
**20:11** *Mary.* Perhaps Jesus appeared first to Mary because she needed him most at that time. *crying.* As in 11:33, it means "wailing," a loud expression of grief.
**20:12** *two angels.* Matthew has one angel (Mt 28:2), Mark a young man (Mk 16:5) and Luke two men who were angels (Lk 24:4,23). See note on Lk 24:4.
**20:14** *did not realize that it was Jesus.* A number of times the risen Jesus was not recognized (21:4; Mt 28:17; Lk 24:16,37). He may have looked different, or he may intentionally have prevented recognition.
**20:16** *Mary.* Cf. 10:3–4. *Rabboni.* A strengthened form of *Rabbi,* and in the NT found elsewhere only in Mk 10:51 (in the Greek). Although the word means "(my) teacher," there are few if any examples of its use in ancient Judaism as a form of address other than in calling on God in prayer. However, John's explanation casts doubt on any thought that Mary intended to address Jesus as God here.
**20:17** *for I have not yet returned.* The meaning appears to be that the ascension was still some time off. Mary would have opportunity to see Jesus again, so she need not cling to him. Alternatively, Jesus may be reminding Mary that after his crucifixion she cannot have him with her except through the Holy Spirit (see 16:5–16). *my brothers.* Probably the disciples (cf. v. 18; Mt 12:50). The members of his family did not believe in him (7:5), though they became disciples not long after this (Ac 1:14). *my Father and your Father.* God is Father both of Christ and of believers, but in different senses

instead to my brothers[c] and tell them, 'I
am returning to my Father[d] and your Father, to my God and your God.' "
18 Mary Magdalene[e] went to the disciples[f] with the news: "I have seen the
Lord!" And she told them that he had said
these things to her.

### *Jesus Appears to His Disciples*

19 On the evening of that first day of the
week, when the disciples were together,
with the doors locked for fear of the
Jews,[g] Jesus came and stood among them
and said, "Peace[h] be with you!"[i] 20 After
he said this, he showed them his hands
and side.[j] The disciples were overjoyed[k]
when they saw the Lord.
21 Again Jesus said, "Peace be with
you![l] As the Father has sent me,[m] I am
sending you."[n] 22 And with that he
breathed on them and said, "Receive the
Holy Spirit.[o] 23 If you forgive anyone his
sins, they are forgiven; if you do not forgive them, they are not forgiven."[p]

### *Jesus Appears to Thomas*

24 Now Thomas[q] (called Didymus), one
of the Twelve, was not with the disciples
when Jesus came. 25 So the other disciples
told him, "We have seen the Lord!"
But he said to them, "Unless I see the
nail marks in his hands and put my finger
where the nails were, and put my hand
into his side,[r] I will not believe it."[s]
26 A week later his disciples were in the
house again, and Thomas was with them.
Though the doors were locked, Jesus came
and stood among them and said, "Peace[t]
be with you!"[u] 27 Then he said to Thomas,
"Put your finger here; see my hands.
Reach out your hand and put it into my
side. Stop doubting and believe."[v]
28 Thomas said to him, "My Lord and
my God!"
29 Then Jesus told him, "Because you
have seen me, you have believed;[w] blessed
are those who have not seen and yet have
believed."[x]
30 Jesus did many other miraculous
signs[y] in the presence of his disciples,
which are not recorded in this book.[z]
31 But these are written that you may[g] believe[a] that Jesus is the Christ, the Son of
God,[b] and that by believing you may have
life in his name.[c]

### *Jesus and the Miraculous Catch of Fish*

21 Afterward Jesus appeared again to
his disciples,[d] by the Sea of Tiberias.[h][e] It happened this way: 2 Simon
Peter, Thomas[f] (called Didymus), Nathanael[g] from Cana in Galilee,[h] the sons
of Zebedee,[i] and two other disciples were
together. 3 "I'm going out to fish," Simon
Peter told them, and they said, "We'll go
with you." So they went out and got into
the boat, but that night they caught nothing.[j]
4 Early in the morning, Jesus stood on

**20:17** [c]S Mt 28:10 [d]Jn 7:33 **20:18** [e]S ver 1 [f]Lk 24:10,22,23 **20:19** [g]S Jn 7:13 [h]S Jn 14:27 [i]ver 21,26; Lk 24:36-39 **20:20** [j]Lk 24:39,40; Jn 19:34 [k]Jn 16:20,22 **20:21** [l]ver 19 [m]S Jn 3:17 [n]Mt 28:19; Jn 17:18 **20:22** [o]Jn 7:39; Ac 2:38; 8:15-17; 19:2; Gal 3:2 **20:23** [p]Mt 16:19; 18:18 **20:24** [q]S Jn 11:16 **20:25** [r]ver 20 [s]Mk 16:11 **20:26** [t]S Jn 14:27 [u]ver 21 **20:27** [v]ver 25; Lk 24:40 **20:29** [w]S Jn 3:15 [x]1Pe 1:8 **20:30** [y]S Jn 2:11 [z]Jn 21:25 **20:31** [a]S Jn 3:15; 19:35 [b]S Mt 4:3 [c]S Mt 25:46 **21:1** [d]ver 14; Jn 20:19,26 [e]Jn 6:1 **21:2** [f]S Jn 11:16 [g]Jn 1:45 [h]Jn 2:1 [i]S Mt 4:21 **21:3** [j]Lk 5:5

[g]*31* Some manuscripts *may continue to* [h]*1* That is, Sea of Galilee

(see 1:12,14,18,34).

**20:19** *disciples.* Probably includes others besides the apostles, "the Twelve" (v. 24). *the Jews.* See note on 1:19. *Peace be with you!* The normal Hebrew greeting (cf. Da 10:19). Because of their behavior the previous Friday, they may have expected rebuke and censure; but Jesus calmed their fears (see note on 14:27).

**20:20** *his hands and side.* Where the wounds were (John does not refer to the wounds in the feet). According to Lk 24:37 they thought they were seeing a ghost. Jesus was clearly identifying himself.

**20:21** *Peace be with you!* See note on v. 19. *I am sending you.* See note on 17:18.

**20:22** *Receive the Holy Spirit.* Thus anticipating what happened 50 days later on the day of Pentecost (Ac 2). The disciples needed God's help to carry out the commission they had just been given.

**20:23** Lit. "Those whose sins you forgive have already been forgiven; those whose sins you do not forgive have not been forgiven." God does not forgive people's sins because we do so, nor does he withhold forgiveness because we do. Rather, those who proclaim the gospel are in effect forgiving or not forgiving sins, depending on whether the hearers accept or reject Jesus Christ.

**20:24** *Thomas.* See note on 11:16.

**20:25** *Unless I see . . . and put . . . I will not believe.* Hardheaded skepticism can scarcely go further than this.

**20:26** *Peace.* See vv. 19,21 and note on 14:27.

**20:28** *My Lord and my God!* The high point of faith (see note on 1:1).

**20:29** *those who have not seen and yet have believed.* Would have been very few at this time. All whom John mentions had seen in some sense. The words, of course, apply to future believers as well.

**20:30** *miraculous signs.* See note on 2:11. John had selected from among many. *in the presence of his disciples.* Those who could testify to what he had done. John again stresses testimony (see note on 1:7).

**20:31** *that you may believe.* Expresses John's evangelistic purpose. *believe.* See note on 1:7. *Jesus is the Christ, the Son of God.* Faith has content. *the Christ.* See note on 1:25. This whole Gospel is written to show the truth of Jesus' Messiahship and to present him as the Son of God, so that the readers may believe in him. *that by believing you may have life.* Another expression of purpose—to bring about faith that leads to life (see notes on 1:4; 3:15). *name.* Represents all that he is and stands for (see note on 2:23).

**21:1** *Sea of Tiberias.* See note on 6:1.

**21:2** *Simon Peter.* See note on Mk 1:16. *Thomas.* See note on 11:16. *sons of Zebedee.* Not named in this Gospel (see Mt 4:21).

**21:3** *that night.* Nighttime was favored by fishermen in ancient times (as Aristotle, e.g., informs us).

**21:4** *did not realize that it was Jesus.* Cf. Mary Magdalene

the shore, but the disciples did not realize
that it was Jesus.[k]
5He called out to them, "Friends,
haven't you any fish?"
"No," they answered.
6He said, "Throw your net on the right
side of the boat and you will find some."
When they did, they were unable to haul
the net in because of the large number of
fish.[l]
7Then the disciple whom Jesus loved[m]
said to Peter, "It is the Lord!" As soon as
Simon Peter heard him say, "It is the
Lord," he wrapped his outer garment
around him (for he had taken it off) and
jumped into the water. 8The other disciples followed in the boat, towing the net
full of fish, for they were not far from
shore, about a hundred yards.[i] 9When
they landed, they saw a fire[n] of burning
coals there with fish on it,[o] and some
bread.
10Jesus said to them, "Bring some of the
fish you have just caught."
11Simon Peter climbed aboard and
dragged the net ashore. It was full of large
fish, 153, but even with so many the net
was not torn. 12Jesus said to them, "Come
and have breakfast." None of the disciples
dared ask him, "Who are you?" They
knew it was the Lord. 13Jesus came, took
the bread and gave it to them, and did the
same with the fish.[p] 14This was now the
third time Jesus appeared to his disciples[q]
after he was raised from the dead.

## *Jesus Reinstates Peter*

15When they had finished eating, Jesus
said to Simon Peter, "Simon son of John,
do you truly love me more than these?"
"Yes, Lord," he said, "you know that I
love you."[r]
Jesus said, "Feed my lambs."[s]
16Again Jesus said, "Simon son of John,
do you truly love me?"
He answered, "Yes, Lord, you know
that I love you."
Jesus said, "Take care of my sheep."[t]
17The third time he said to him, "Simon
son of John, do you love me?"
Peter was hurt because Jesus asked him
the third time, "Do you love me?"[u] He
said, "Lord, you know all things;[v] you
know that I love you."
Jesus said, "Feed my sheep.[w] 18I tell you
the truth, when you were younger you
dressed yourself and went where you
wanted; but when you are old you will
stretch out your hands, and someone else
will dress you and lead you where you do
not want to go." 19Jesus said this to indicate the kind of death[x] by which Peter
would glorify God.[y] Then he said to him,
"Follow me!"[z]
20Peter turned and saw that the disciple
whom Jesus loved[a] was following them.
(This was the one who had leaned back
against Jesus at the supper and had said,
"Lord, who is going to betray you?")[b]
21When Peter saw him, he asked, "Lord,
what about him?"
22Jesus answered, "If I want him to remain alive until I return,[c] what is that to
you? You must follow me."[d] 23Because of

**21:4** [k]Lk 24:16; Jn 20:14 **21:6** [l]Lk 5:4-7 **21:7** [m]S Jn 13:23 **21:9** [n]Jn 18:18 [o]ver 10,13 **21:13** [p]ver 9 **21:14** [q]Jn 20:19, 26
**21:15** [r]Mt 26:33, 35; Jn 13:37 [s]Lk 12:32 **21:16** [t]2Sa 5:2; Eze 34:2; Mt 2:6; S Jn 10:11; Ac 20:28; 1Pe 5:2,3 **21:17** [u]Jn 13:38 [v]Jn 16:30 [w]S ver 16 **21:19** [x]Jn 12:33; 18:32 [y]Jn 13:36; 2Pe 1:14 [z]S Mt 4:19 **21:20** [a]ver 7; S Jn 13:23 [b]Jn 13:25 **21:22** [c]S Mt 16:27 [d]ver 19; S Mt 4:19

[i]8 Greek *about two hundred cubits* (about 90 meters)

(see note on 20:14).
**21:7** *disciple whom Jesus loved.* See note on 13:23. *his outer garment.* It is curious that he put on this garment (the word appears only here in the NT) preparatory to jumping into the water. But Jews regarded a greeting as a religious act that could be done only when one was clothed. Peter may have been preparing himself to greet the Lord.
**21:9** *burning coals.* Lit. "charcoal," as in 18:18 ("fire"; see note on 18:26).
**21:11** *Peter . . . dragged the net ashore.* Appears to mean that Peter headed up the effort, for the whole group had not been able previously to haul the net into the boat (v. 6). *the net was not torn.* In contrast to the nets mentioned in Lk 5:6.
**21:14** *the third time.* The third appearance to a group of disciples (20:19–23,24–29), though there had been other appearances to individuals.
**21:15–17** *love.* The Greek word for "love" in Jesus' first two questions is different from that in his third question and in all Peter's answers. It is uncertain whether a distinction in meaning is intended since John often made slight word variations, apparently for stylistic reasons. Also, no distinction is made between these two words elsewhere in this Gospel. In this passage, however, they occur together, and the variations seem too deliberate to be explained on stylistic grounds. "Truly love" refers to a love in which the entire personality, including the will, is involved. "Love" refers to spontaneous natural affection or fondness in which emotion plays a more prominent role than will. Whatever interpretation is adopted, the important thing is that in so serious a matter as the reinstatement of Peter, the great question was whether he loved Jesus.
**21:15** *more than these.* May mean "more than you love these men" or "more than these men love me" or "more than you love these things" (i.e., the fishing gear). Perhaps the second is best, for Peter had claimed a devotion above that of the others (cf. 13:37; Mt 26:33; Mk 14:29). Peter did not take up the comparison, and Jesus did not explain it. *Feed my lambs.* Probably means much the same as "Take care of my sheep" (v. 16) and "Feed my sheep" (v. 17).
**21:17** *you know all things.* Peter's replies stress Christ's knowledge, not his own grasp of the situation.
**21:18** *stretch out your hands.* The early church understood this as a prophecy of crucifixion.
**21:19** *the kind of death.* Peter would be a martyr. Tradition indicates that he was crucified upside down.
**21:20** *disciple whom Jesus loved.* See note on 13:23. *was following.* He was doing what Peter was twice told to do (vv. 19,22). *at the supper.* See 13:23–25.
**21:22** *until I return.* A clear declaration of the second

this, the rumor spread among the brothers[e] that this disciple would not die. But Jesus did not say that he would not die; he only said, "If I want him to remain alive until I return, what is that to you?"
24This is the disciple who testifies to these things[f] and who wrote them down. We know that his testimony is true.[g]
25Jesus did many other things as well.[h] If every one of them were written down, I suppose that even the whole world would not have room for the books that would be written.

**21:23** [e]S Ac 1:16
**21:24** [f]S Jn 15:27 [g]Jn 19:35
**21:25** [h]Jn 20:30

coming.
**21:24** *disciple who testifies.* Testimony is important throughout this Gospel (see note on 1:7). We now learn that it was the beloved disciple who was the witness behind the account. *these things.* Must refer to the whole book. *who wrote them down.* The beloved disciple was not only the witness but also the actual author. *We know.* Evidently written by contemporaries in a position to know the truth.
**21:25** *many other things.* As in 20:30 we are assured that the author has been selective. *even the whole world would not have room.* Our historical knowledge of Jesus is at best partial, but we have been given all we need to know.